# Modeling Mary

## in Christian Discipleship

# Modeling Mary
## in Christian Discipleship

JOHN BURNS

JUDSON PRESS
PUBLISHERS SINCE 1824
VALLEY FORGE, PA

# Modeling Mary in Christian Discipleship

Judson Press has made every effort to trace the ownership of all quotes. In the event of a question arising from the use of a quote, we regret any error made and will be pleased to make the necessary correction in future printings and editions of this book.

Bible quotations in this volume are from the New Revised Standard Version of the Bible, copyright © 1989 by the Division of Christian Education of the National Council of the Churches of Christ in the United States of America. Used by permission. All rights reserved.

Library of Congress Cataloging-in-Publication Data

Burns, John Phillip, 1956-
Modeling Mary in Christian discipleship / John Phillip Burns. — 1st ed.
p. cm.
ISBN 978-0-8170-1514-5 (pbk. : alk. paper) 1. Mary, Blessed Virgin, Saint. I. Title.
BT603.B87 2007
232.91—dc22

2007002845

Printed on recycled paper in the U.S.A.

First Edition, 2007.

To my children,
Josh, Micah, Aaron, Jacob, and Joanna,
my daughter-in-law, Jessica,
and my grandson, Cyrus.
They are all in this book somewhere,
and each has taught me something
about being a disciple of Christ.
Most importantly, to my wife, Karen,
whose artistry in following Christ
exceeds all others I have known.

# CONTENTS

# ACKNOWLEDGMENTS

I can no longer separate out the various strands of teaching, modeling, and sharing that have woven the tapestry of this book. My parents provided the initial threads. Although more of a "behind the scenes" follower of Christ, my father practiced his faith with honesty, integrity, and sincere devotion. I learned how to be honest about my faith from him. My mother, as I have noted in these pages, continues to the serve the Lord with panache and passion. As she does everything else in life, she expresses her love for Christ from the heart with both exuberance and pathos. She has taught me to prize highly the contribution of women in the life of the church.

My two brothers and sister, Stephen, David, and Cathy, and my sister's husband, Jim, have paralleled my own journey of discipleship. When I have fallen to difficult lows, they have always been there to pray for me, comfort me, and love me until I was able to get up and travel again. When I have risen to pursue the high calling of our Lord, they have celebrated with me.

My children, Josh, Micah, Aaron, Jacob, and Joanna, as well as my daughter-in-law, Jessica, and my grandson, Cyrus, have each taught me lessons in discipleship. Sometimes they have challenged me to grow up; other times they have pushed me to take my faith seriously enough to practice it during the stresses of parenting, and most often they have reflected back to me God's love, grace, and truth.

My wife, Karen, has taught me the meaning of grace and kindness. She has a maturity and purity to her faith that informs and inspires my own.

Many teachers have provided the tools I use to study and interpret Scripture. I want to make special mention of Dr. Paul Travis who, as a history professor at Oklahoma Baptist University, was the first adult to challenge me with the social justice implications of the Bible. I also am grateful for all the professors in biblical studies from whom I benefited at the New Orleans Baptist Theological Seminary. Most recently, I received new perspective on Mary, the mother of Jesus, from a course I took under Richard Rohr and Ronald Rolheiser at Boston College in the summer of 2005.

There are too many friends and colleagues to thank inclusively. But surely my old friends Buzz Thomas, Robert Dibble, Jack Averill, Mark McIntyre, and Jean Robinson Casey have influenced my understanding of life and the New Testament in very positive ways. These days I am constantly supported, advised, and encouraged by Jay Stearns, Chris Holmes, Steve Larsen, Mark Smiley, Bob Jordan, David Jordan, and Terry Minchow-Proffitt, who meet with me each month and keep me grounded in the grace of our Lord.

This book would not have happened without my friend Curtis Ramsey-Lucas who felt strongly enough about the content to make sure a publisher considered it. I am deeply indebted to him.

Rebecca Irwin-Diehl, the editor of this book, has given me superb direction and clarity. I tend to paint in large strokes; she helped refine and define the picture.

Last, but possibly of most importance, has been the contribution of the church I currently serve. The University Baptist Church of College Park, Maryland, has loved me through the best and worst of my life. Throughout too many episodes to describe here, they have continued to affirm my calling, my gifts, and my contribution to the kingdom of God. They continued to see the hand of God in me when I had almost lost sight of it myself. I could not have developed this book if they had not affirmed the content and encouraged the effort involved. Some of them provided the best stories in the book as well. I will live the rest of my life indebted to the disciples who call themselves the University Baptist Church.

# 1

# MARY

## A Nonlinear View of Discipleship

My name is John Philip Burns. I tell you this so that you'll know that I was named after John Philip Sousa, the renowned composer of marching band music. From the day of my birth, my mother had hopes that I would become a great musician. And that's why when I was a boy, my least favorite day of school was Friday.

I know that's a little odd, because most children my age thanked God when it was Friday—the beginning of the weekend. Friday night was a game night, movie night, stay-up-late night, no-homework night. For me, however, Friday was "challenge day" in band.

Monday through Thursday, all of the band concentrated on playing together to produce beautiful symphonic sounds. The only challenge before us throughout the week was playing the notes in concert and mastering the piece. When one kid played his or her instrument well, we all celebrated. We encouraged one another to do well, complimented one another's stellar achievements, and forgave one another the sour notes that invariably wriggled out of the instruments of young musicians.

But on Friday, that spirit of harmony and goodwill evaporated. We arrived in the band room wary of one another. No longer were we collaborating on a piece of music. On Friday, we were competing for the best chairs in our sections. I played the trumpet and seemed always to be stuck in third chair. The boys ahead of me were better trumpeters than I was. They practiced harder, incorporated the fundamentals better, and cared more about being in first chair than I did.

I was quite happy residing in third chair, but my mother felt otherwise about my position (remember the name thing). She believed that her children should be the best at whatever they tried to master, so every Friday she pushed me to challenge the guy in second chair. This meant that he and I each had to play the same piece of music while our band director listened. Then the director would decide who had performed the piece with the highest skill. If I performed better than the second-chair player (which almost never happened), I moved up and he moved down. If not, I stayed in third chair for another week. If I lost the challenge, I felt no great pain. As I said, I liked third chair. It seemed to be a just appraisal of my talent. However, something close to terror arose in me when the kid in fourth chair got a notion to challenge me.

The guy in fourth chair didn't take band seriously at all. He was the kid who ingeniously used his trumpet to make animal-like noises or even less appropriate sounds in order to make the girls in the clarinet section laugh. He rarely if ever practiced, paid the shoddiest attention to the fundamentals, and couldn't have cared less about which chair he occupied. However, from time to time, because he was so loose and nonchalant about the exercise, he played the "challenge piece" with greater ease than I did. The band director would listen and then tell us to switch places. I felt no great shame returning home on Fridays to tell my mom that I was still in third chair, but I felt utter humiliation when I, John

Phillip, had to report that I had fallen to fourth chair. I could hear the composer of "The Stars and Stripes Forever" quietly sobbing in marching band heaven.

"Challenge day" is probably what caused me to hate being placed in categories based on achievement. I loved playing my trumpet. I actually got a thrill out of helping to produce the sound that our symphonic and marching bands united to perform. If it were not for the hideous "chair" system, which kept putting pressure on me to rise to the next level of proficiency, band would have been my favorite class. But as it was, I dreaded the end of each week and eventually came to dislike playing the trumpet entirely.

Partly because of this experience, I have always had a strong aversion to descriptions of discipleship that involve gradations of achievement. Many best-selling publications on discipleship indicate that there are steps for disciples to follow that will take us from a beginner's level of devotion all the way up to a mastery of the discipline. Some authors say that there are five steps, others six or seven or ten. Writers call these steps "stages" or "phases" or "levels" of Christian maturity. Although the terminology differs from guide to guide, the general teaching remains the same: people move in a direct line from baptism to sainthood, ascending the rungs of the discipleship ladder.

This prevalent framework has caused me to wonder which step I am on. I was baptized decades ago, so by now I should be quite far along the journey to maturity. I have asked myself if I am working on the appropriate level for my age, training, and experience. Have I at long last reached second chair, or have I risen quickly to occupy third chair and been stuck there for years? Am I an advanced student of Jesus, or am I a little behind the curve? Have I reached the high school of faith, or did the Spirit send me back to repeat a grade due to insufficient progress?

My honest answer seems to vary from day to day. On occasion I have been amazingly mature in my response to an insult, truly compassionate in the face of human need, and bold in my ability to share my faith. Unfortunately, there have been many other days when I have folded to even the smallest challenge to the ways of Christ. Looking back over time, I can see that I have grown some from the day of my conversion, but I cannot plot an ascending graph of my progress. In fact, the rise and fall of the stock market would more closely resemble my journey toward Christian maturity. I have often wondered if I was the only believer who couldn't definitively locate myself in the stages of faith. Was I the only Christian who didn't know whether he was on level two, three, or four?

These questions disturbed me until I examined the lives of the followers of Jesus as depicted in Scripture. To my relief, I wasn't sure I could see uninterrupted linear progress in their discipleship either. Peter began promisingly and made rapid progress in following Jesus. But then he regressed into brash episodes of arrogance and pride. One moment he was testifying that although all other disciples might leave Jesus in his hour of need, he would stay true. But in the next heartbeat, Peter succumbed to the relatively minor pressure of a servant girl and denied Jesus three times.

Peter rose to the occasion on Pentecost and preached powerfully. However, even after that mighty sermon he still showed a demeaning attitude toward people who didn't happen to have been born Jewish. Of course, that problem was dealt with on the rooftop of Simon the tanner's home in Joppa, and Peter was off and running again, vining up the trellis of Christian maturity—until some of his Jewish buddies put pressure on him. The lead apostle then reverted to a beginner's level of maturity and refused to eat with his Gentile friends while his Jewish friends were watching. When we take stock of the scriptural account of Peter's life, we're not sure which stage of discipleship he achieved.

The apostle John might serve as an example of a disciple who made more predictable progress toward spiritual maturity. He came to Christ as a young man and developed until he reached old age. But even after achieving the status of a Christian elder, John continued to refer to himself in the rather self-promoting way as the "disciple whom Jesus loved." Doesn't that indicate a stubborn sense of self-importance that should have been eradicated before reaching the final stage of Christian maturity? The apostle Paul likewise had some struggles with arrogance. There are more than a few clues in his writings that the pomposity that was fed by his pharisaical background possibly persisted long after his Damascus Road conversion.

Which step were these men on? Had they each achieved the midlevel of discipleship? Were they three-quarters of the way to the top? Were they above or below timberline on the mountain slope of spiritual maturity? As I struggled with these observations, I began to wonder if there was a better way of talking about discipleship than as a journey through various stages and levels of growth. The fact is that grading people on a chart of spiritual maturity makes the grader feel either smugly superior to other Christian brothers or sisters ("I'm on level eight, you are still obviously on level four") or shamefully inferior ("No matter what I do, I just can't shake off the self-centeredness of level three"). Neither attitude is encouraged by Jesus.

Grading myself didn't seem to be appropriate in other significant areas of my life, so why, I pondered, was it a part of my spiritual life? I believe that I have grown as a father (there are five children in this world who may beg to differ) and as a husband (one very gracious wife might have to bite her lip), but I never try to assess whether I have arrived at level four of fatherhood or have achieved the final stage of spousal maturity. To measure something so personal, dynamic, and intimate is impossible. The same can be said of measuring one's growth in discipleship.

I began to wonder whether discipleship might be more like learning an art form than like advancing up the chairs of the trumpet section in the school band. One of my hobbies is writing songs. I'm not a working songwriter. I've never earned a penny for any of my compositions. Rather, I'm a practicing songwriter. Every year I write two or three songs. Sometimes I compare a recent composition with one that I wrote years ago to see if I'm making progress as a songwriter. On some days it appears that I am, but on other days it seems that I am regressing. Sometimes the melody and turn of phrase that I incorporated into one of my first attempts at songwriting seems fresher and less contrived than a lyric or tune I just finished. In general, I believe that I am growing as a songwriter, but I can't tell you which stage of songwriting I am on. That's because the practice of an art form is more dynamic than it is linear. So too, I believe, is the journey of discipleship.

Over time, we ought to be able to see that our love and service for Jesus Christ are deepening. However, this realization is probably more like the recognition of a painter who sees that she has painted a picture with a richness of texture and color that she would not have been able to achieve a few years back. I think that it's less like the awareness of a brown belt in karate who is told that he is now ready to move on to black.

Artists are people who are connected to a source of inspiration that enables them to create and express beauty and truth in ways that often confound even themselves. Although artists must work hard to cultivate their abilities, they more often refer to these abilities as gifts rather than achievements. The best artists stand in awe of the grace that has enabled them to create their masterpieces.

I am led to believe that it is the same with discipleship. To be a disciple of Jesus Christ is to be connected with an inspiration beyond ourselves that empowers us to become more like Jesus than we ever thought possible. Growth in discipleship takes work and discipline to nourish the new life within us, but that nourishment rarely produces a feeling of pride. Instead, the longer we follow Jesus, the more aware we become that any resemblance we have to Christ is due solely to the grace of God.

Rather than trumpet the advanced stage of discipleship that we've earned, we simply grow more in awe of this grace that allows us to be called followers of Jesus.

After I arrived at this understanding of discipleship, I began to look for a follower of Jesus whose life illustrated this dynamic, artistic approach to spiritual maturity. Somewhat to my surprise, the disciple I was most drawn to was Mary, the mother of Jesus. I saw in Mary a woman who began her masterpiece in discipleship with a keen understanding of grace and nurtured that gift through the ups and downs of her spiritual growth. Mary's progress toward spiritual maturity cannot be plotted with a smoothly ascending line on a graph. The experiences that shaped Mary's spiritual development seem to be more like colors and hues of an artist's palette than like rungs on a spiritual ladder. Mary learned something through every encounter she had with Jesus, tragic or euphoric. Whether she responded with maturity or immaturity, trust or anxiety, wisdom or ignorance, she grew. Each new understanding added richness to the palette, so that by the end of her story, as we know it, she was demonstrating exceptional devotion to Jesus.

I still don't know what step of discipleship I am on. I don't even try to figure it out anymore. My prayer is that I will continue to receive the grace necessary to grow as a follower of Christ. Mary's life has helped me to see all the episodes of my life as material that God uses to create a mature disciple. There are times when I soar to awesome heights as a follower of Christ, and there are times when I plummet to embarrassing lows—God uses both to create a life that a little more closely resembles the one whom I follow.

I offer these reflections on the life of the mother of Jesus in the hope that you will come to see more of the grace of God in your own life. Maybe you too will find that it's not as important for you to document your own current stage of discipleship as it is to stand in awe of God's ability to use all the experiences of your life, good and bad, to create a mature follower of Jesus Christ.

## Questions for Reflection

1. How would you depict your journey of discipleship? Have you experienced continual progress up the ladder of spiritual maturity? If not, how would you describe your spiritual growth so far?

2. Instead of picturing your walk of discipleship as an upward movement through various levels, try thinking of it as a work of art. What experiences so far have given you the hues necessary to paint your current acts of love and service for Christ?

3. Who has provided a helpful model of discipleship for your life? What has this person taught you about following Jesus? Has this person ascended smoothly upward through various stages of spiritual maturity, or has his or her journey of discipleship had some ups and downs?

4. What part does grace play in your spiritual growth?

# 2

# EXCHANGING AGENDAS WITH GOD:
## The Beginning of Discipleship

## Luke 1:26-38

*In the sixth month the angel Gabriel was sent by God to a town in Galilee called Nazareth, to a virgin engaged to a man whose name was Joseph, of the house of David. The virgin's name was Mary. And he came to her and said, "Greetings, favored one! The Lord is with you." But she was much perplexed by his words and pondered what sort of greeting this might be. The angel said to her, "Do not be afraid, Mary, for you have found favor with God. And now, you will conceive in your womb and bear a son, and you will name him Jesus. He will be great, and will be called the Son of the Most High, and the Lord God will give to him the throne of his ancestor David. He will reign over the house of Jacob forever, and of his kingdom there will be no end." Mary said to the angel, "How can this be, since I am a virgin?" The angel said to her, "The Holy Spirit will come upon you, and the power of the Most High will overshadow you;*

*therefore the child to be born will be holy; he will be called Son of God. And now, your relative Elizabeth in her old age has also conceived a son; and this is the sixth month for her who was said to be barren. For nothing will be impossible with God." Then Mary said, "Here am I, the servant of the Lord; let it be with me according to your word." Then the angel departed from her.*

Every disciple has a moment in time when he or she accepts the call to follow Jesus. This moment of spiritual commitment may be preceded by weeks, months, even years of consideration. A person can be an admirer of Jesus without ever saying yes to the call, but not a disciple. One can be a good member of the community, a reliable employee, a loving family member, and even a decent neighbor without saying yes to the call, but not a disciple. At some point, if we are to become disciples of Jesus Christ, we have to make a holy decision to follow him. The precise details of how a disciple accepts the call of Christ and begins the journey of discipleship vary from person to person. But in every case the starting point involves an exchange of agendas between the disciple and Christ.

When I entered college, I had every intention of pursuing a degree in music and serving God as a church musician. There were a few hitches to my plan, however. The biggest hitch was that I wasn't a musician. Trying not to let a small detail like that get in the way of my agenda, I entered Oklahoma Baptist University in the fall of 1974 as a music major. Since I couldn't play any instrument well, I declared that I would focus my studies on vocal performance. I was therefore assigned to a teacher who was to help train my voice to sing the praises of God.

My instructor was an older woman nearing retirement. She sat in a chair, coached me, and sighed in frustration—a lot. As the semester came to a close, she required that I sing in the class recital. We rehearsed an Italian number entitled "Vittorio." I tried to learn it. I really did. I practiced and practiced, but it was in Italian. I didn't speak Italian. So when it was my turn to sing in the recital, I stood and sang the word "Vittorio" nine times in a row. There were many more words in the song, but I couldn't remember them. As I burst forth with my tenth "Vittorio," I noticed that the kindly professor had placed her head in her hands.

The next semester I was passed on to another vocal instructor. After only one lesson, my new professor sat down beside me and played a very complicated vocal piece on the piano. He asked me to sing the first line. I couldn't sing the first note. He said, "John, if you continue pursuing a music degree, for the next two years you will be required to sing music like this. Is this really what you want to do?" God was changing my agenda.

Mary of Nazareth must have been very excited about her immediate plans. She was engaged to marry Joseph, a good man from a great family. Her future husband could trace his genetic roots all the way back to Israel's only true superstar, the mighty King David. Mary must have been thankful that her family had accomplished all the transactions necessary to secure a marriage with such a desirable man. Other young women her age were not so fortunate.

Surely her mind was filled with wedding plans. Although neither her family nor Joseph's was wealthy, a wedding was the one occasion when even peasant families threw a festive party. There would have been a menu to organize, garments to make, invitations to send, musicians to recruit, and relatives to gather. I don't think that Mary focused all her thoughts solely on the wedding itself. I believe that she also contemplated the meaning of the sacred covenant that she was about to make with Joseph. Mary, no doubt, thought through what it was going to be like to share her life with this good man, to work as partners to build a life, to exchange love and affection, and one day to raise a family. She must have been gratified to see that everything she had hoped for was unfolding according to her plan.

Mary's agenda was good, healthy, and appropriate for her age and time. But God had a different mission for her. God's design for Mary's life was announced by the angel Gabriel, who said, "Greetings, Mary. You have found favor with God. The Lord is with you. Now you will conceive in your womb and bear a son, and you will name him Jesus." *Now!* She must have thought, "No, not now! Down the road, after the proper engagement, after the wedding, after Joseph and I have settled into our home, then it will be time for a baby." Mary's plan called for a baby then, not now. Gabriel continued to speak of God's plan, however. "This child of yours will be called the Son of the Most High, and the Lord God will give to him the throne of his ancestor David. He will reign over the house of Jacob forever."

"Mother of a king," Mary might have said to herself. "Wow, that is really something. Much more than I ever expected, really. I always thought it would be enough just to have healthy children who showed me respect and affection. But a mother of a king—well, that would be quite a privilege. However, now is definitely not the time."

Although we can't know all that was going on inside Mary's mind, we do know that she expressed understandable confusion at the timing of the angel's message. "How can this be," she inquired, "since I am still a virgin?" I can easily picture Mary saying, "Gabriel, what you describe is genuinely a tremendous opportunity, and I am happy to be considered for this wondrous honor. But you see, I can't become the mother of a king right now. I'm still a virgin. There is no baby in my immediate future. Believe me, I think I would know. Why don't you come back in a few years, and then we will talk. Your agenda for my life, as wonderful as it is, just doesn't fit into my plan right now." But Gabriel plowed on through the message. "The Holy Spirit will come upon you. And the power of the Most High will overshadow you; therefore the child will be born, and he will be called the Son of God."

Exchanging our plans for those of another is a stiff challenge for most of us. That's precisely why we don't always answer the phone when it rings. We know that if we answer it, we will have to exchange our agenda with that of the caller. If we are in the midst of eating dinner, watching TV, playing with our kids, or fixing a leaky faucet, we just let the phone ring because we are unwilling to allow our attention to be redirected to the caller's priorities. If Mary could have screened Gabriel's call, she might not have picked up, but she didn't have that luxury. Instead, she had to decide whether she was willing to exchange her well-thought-out intentions for the surprising plan that God had for her life. The decision that faced Mary is the first decision confronted by all would-be disciples. God calls, and we have to decide whether we are going to ignore God's prompting and stay with our own carefully conceived plans or whether we are willing to exchange what we thought we were going to do with our lives for the mission that God has for us.

Evangelists had a profound effect on my early spiritual development. Twice a year, an evangelist came to the church of my youth and conducted a seven-day revival. I liked all the services of the revival, but my favorite was always "youth night." On "youth night" every teenager in the church was challenged to bring friends to the revival. We were promised pizza and games and prizes if we brought classmates and neighbors and kids from our baseball team to hear the great preacher speak a message "especially attuned to the needs of our youth." This "especially attuned" message always involved the evangelist's personal witness of how the Lord saved him. The testimony invariably began with a prolonged narrative of all the rotten things the preacher had done before he met Jesus. This was the part of the sermon that captured our fertile minds. Tales of drug and alcohol abuse, sexual promiscuity, wild parties, dangerous activities, shady friendships, and reckless monetary expenditures ignited our imaginations of what it meant to promenade down the wide, winding avenue of sin rather than march along the straight and narrow road of Baptist devotion. Eventually, the evangelist would tell of his encounter with the Lord and how that experience helped him see the error of his ways and start his new life with Christ. I don't think that the sincere preachers knew that many of us who were racing toward adolescence harbored secret desires to get started on the first part of our testimonies. We were convinced that someday we too would want to get saved from the ultimate consequences of our prodigal lives, but first we wanted to experience a little of the waywardness that the flashy evangelist seemed to know so well.

The dramatic conversion testimonies of these evangelists left me with a belief that "flashy sinners," not "respectable normal people," had to exchange agendas with Christ in order to become disciples. I used to think that folks who lied, cheated, partied, used profanity, skipped church, and ran around with others who did likewise needed to exchange agendas with Jesus. On the other hand, I was sure that folks who held down jobs, came home every night to their families, abstained from excesses of every kind, and used good manners in public were pretty much on the same page with Jesus already.

That's why I find Mary's call to discipleship so helpful. Mary was respectable in every way. Nothing in the biblical text gives us any hint that she was anything other than a devout young woman from an excellent family with a solid reputation. If Gabriel had visited the Samaritan woman at the well with the request to become the mother of Jesus, or the woman caught in adultery, or even Mary Magdalene, then we would have had another example of a person with an inappropriate pedigree or checkered past who was redeemed by the love of Christ. Such stories are important and transforming, but they are not the story of Mary, the mother of Jesus. Her story is of one who was living about as well-managed a life as one could live. Nothing in her future plans was inappropriate or sinful. And yet even she had to exchange agendas with God in order to begin her life as a disciple of Christ.

Mary's journey of discipleship teaches that each of us, regardless of whether we have destructive desires or noble goals for our lives, must defer those plans to the ways of Jesus if we are going to become disciples. For what makes these plans obstacles to discipleship is not so much their particulars as it is the process by which we make them. Before we answer the call of discipleship, we set our agenda based upon what seems best to us. We use the standards of wisdom that we have received from family, friends, and culture. Once we decide to become a disciple of Jesus, however, we have to turn over the management of this process to him. In other words, we have to ask Christ what he wants for our lives. For disciples, the agenda that Jesus has for our life takes precedence over anything that we plan for ourselves.

Unfortunately, we often try to claim discipleship to Jesus without making this exchange. Instead, we try to negotiate with God to get divine blessing on our own plans. Much of what is preached under the heading of "prosperity gospel" is simply encouragement to get God to help make our personal endeavors pay off. "Believe in God, and your bank account will grow." "Seek God's blessing, and your business will thrive." These promises have nothing to do with discipleship. Discipleship does not even begin until we are willing to exchange our goals for the mission that God has for our lives. If Mary had been under the sway of modern "prosperity gospel" preachers, she might have responded to Gabriel's invitation by saying, "I'm really not interested in getting on board with God's mysterious will, but I could use a little divine help in planning my wedding. Lord, Joseph's uncle Benjamin has a lot of money. Do you think you could get him to send a little of it our way? My figure has been expanding of late. Do you think you could help me trim down for the big day? The wedding will be outside. Do you think you could send us some pretty weather for the festivities?"

As silly as these sentiments sound, they are not all that far off from the prayers that we often take to God. We all fall into the trap of trying to get God to endorse our plans rather than yielding our agendas to the lordship of Christ. When Gabriel pronounced God's plan for Mary, she had to decide whether she was willing to yield her right to orchestrate her own future to the lordship of Christ. What if she had responded by saying, "No, thank you for thinking of me, Lord, but I think I'll pass. I have things all set just the way I want them." We have the option to resist and even reject God's plans for us; theologians call it "free will." There are thousands of ways to live the one life we have. Discipleship is just one way. So why should we turn over the reins of our lives to God rather than continue with our well-crafted strategies for success?

In 1927 the Mississippi River jumped its banks in Cairo, Illinois, and flooded hundreds of thousands of acres all the way down to New Orleans. The town of Greenville, Mississippi, was one of the areas hardest hit. When the floodwaters rose in that little Southern town, every person with a boat was conscripted into rescuing survivors. John Tigrett was only fourteen years old at the time. He had a small boat with an outboard motor, so he helped in the lifesaving mission.

Tigrett motored about forty-five minutes from dry ground when he saw three people perched on a rooftop. When he stopped for the stranded evacuees, one of the women informed him that she was about to deliver a baby. John knew that they were forty-five minutes from medical help, so he asked the woman if she could hold on until he could get her professional attention. The poor woman said that she couldn't wait, because the baby was on the way. Under duress, John consented to help with the delivery. The expectant mother told him exactly what to do, and within a very short time, the young boy was holding the newborn infant in his arms. The amazing experience moved Tigrett to tears.[1]

John Tigrett had very good intentions for his day. He set out to rescue people stranded by a monstrous flood. But the woman had another priority. The young boy had to decide whether or not to set aside his important agenda for her even more urgent one. He decided to make the exchange, and when he did, he participated in the birthing of a new life.

Mary had to decide whether she was willing to exchange her agenda for God's. Would she set aside her very good plans and willingly give birth to the Son of God at this very surprising time in her life? Or would she stay the course with all that she had envisioned for her life and reject this commission from God? After serious reflection, Mary said yes to God. She replied, "Here I am, the servant of the Lord; let it be according to your word." And as a result of her willingness to exchange agendas with God, Mary began her journey of discipleship. A journey that very quickly included giving birth to the Son of God.

Why would any of us take this first step of discipleship? Why would any of us exchange the well-laid plans that we have for our lives for the plans drawn up in the heart of God? Because when we exchange our plans for the mission of God, we find that we too participate in giving birth to Christ in our own time. As we begin to live out God's intentions for our lives, people start seeing Jesus in us. We reveal the love of Christ in the way we care for our family, our neighbors, our workmates, and our friends. We demonstrate the compassion of Christ as we respond to the needs of the hungry, homeless, estranged, and lonely. We incarnate the peace of Christ as we respond to insult with blessing, hatred with love, and violence with forgiveness. We bring forth the devotion of Christ as we worship, pray, meditate, and praise God. We exhibit the contentment of Christ as we turn away from rampant materialism and find deep joy in more modest lifestyles. We manifest the power of Christ as we confront racism, work for justice, witness for peace, cry out for integrity, and defy the destructive powers of our generation. We unleash the hope of

Christ as we share the good news of salvation with the people of our lives.

The privilege of giving birth to the presence of Christ in our own times is a wondrous, beautiful, and profound experience. As Mary understood, to be involved in such a miracle is worth giving up anything else that we had planned to do with our lives.

## Questions for Reflection

1. What dreams might Mary have had for her life before Gabriel made his miraculous announcement? What were some of your dreams when you were younger?

2. What kind of inner conversation did Mary have with herself as she contemplated how to respond to Gabriel's message? What did she risk losing if she exchanged agendas with God? What did she stand to gain by such an exchange?

3. Why do we prefer to seek God's blessing for our own plans rather than exchange our plans for the agenda of God? Why does God ask us to make this exchange? What plans for your life are you most reluctant to give up at this time?

4. What excites you about the commission to give birth to Christ in your generation? Where would you like to be involved in revealing the life of Jesus in our world today? Would such involvement be worth giving up the plans that you have made for your life so far? Why or why not?

# 3

# CONVERSION EUPHORIA
## The Initial Rush of Discipleship

Luke 1:46-56

*And Mary said, "My soul magnifies the Lord, and my spirit rejoices in God my Savior, for he has looked with favor on the lowliness of his servant. Surely from now on all generations will call me blessed; for the Mighty One has done great things for me, and holy is his name. His mercy is for those who fear him from generation to generation. He has shown strength with his arm; he has scattered the proud in the thoughts of their hearts. He has brought down the powerful from their thrones, and lifted up the lowly; he has filled the hungry with good things, and sent the rich away empty. He has helped his servant Israel, in remembrance of his mercy, according to the promise he made to our ancestors, to Abraham and to his descendants forever." And Mary remained with her about three months and then returned to her home.*

Several years ago, one of my sons was going through a tough time, and I was going through it with him. He had responded to the painful realities of his life with a series of poor choices. I, along with others, tried several responses to his actions in the hope that something might help him make healthier decisions. One of those responses was to attend counseling with him. For a brief period, it looked as if the therapy was helping us both and that he had learned his lessons and was making wiser choices. Then, as I drove him to our third counseling session, he informed me of his most recent, infuriating mistake.

As he talked to the counselor alone about what he had done, I sat outside the office fuming. Beside me sat my son's ever-present girlfriend. My mental replay of all my son's foolish behavior was interrupted by her voice. She said, "Mr. Burns, your son is so smart. He can do anything he sets his mind to do. And he is such a hard worker. He's doing great in his new job. I think that his boss loves him more than I do. I'd trust him with any problem that I have because he is just that smart." I thought, *No wonder my son listens to this girl more than he does to me. All she can see are his good qualities.* That's the way it is in the initial stages of romance: we register only the strengths of our new love. In *The Road Less Traveled*, M. Scott Peck notes what happens when we fall in love: "We believe that the strength of our love will cause the forces of opposition to bow down in submission and melt away into the darkness. All problems will be overcome. The future will be all light."[1]

Mary fell in love with the Lord after her life-changing encounter with the angel Gabriel. In the initial moments following her decision to embrace God's plan and become the mother of Jesus, all she could see were the positive aspects of her new relationship with God. Her feelings were so powerful that she couldn't hold them in, and she burst into song. Mary sang, "My spirit rejoices in God my Savior." Then, in a cavalcade of exuberant exclamations, Mary said, "All generations will call me blessed… the Mighty One has done great things for me…his mercy is for those who fear him…he has shown strength with his arm…he has scattered the proud…brought down the powerful…lifted up the lowly…filled the hungry…helped his servant Israel," all in keeping with his promises. From her mountaintop of euphoric emotion, Mary couldn't see any problem with serving the Lord and carrying out his will. All was light, good, positive, cheerful.

Contrast Mary's song with the words uttered by Job when he was at quite a different place in life. In the twenty-fourth chapter of his misery, Job described the plight of the needy in this world. After calling attention to their suffering, Job said, "From the city the dying groan, and the throat of the wounded cries for help; yet God pays no attention to their prayer." Job concluded his observation of the unfairness of this world by saying that the corrupt and merciless got away with all sorts of atrocities and that "God prolongs the life of the mighty by his power." Then he ended his expression of outrage by saying, "If it is not so, who will prove me a liar, and show that there is nothing in what I say?" (Job 24:12,22a,25).

Which person, Mary or Job, stated the whole truth about life in this world? Are we guaranteed nothing but success as we follow the Lord? Or are we doomed to heartbreak and exasperation in the face of the horrors that go on under the watchful eye of God? Your answer probably depends on what is happening in your life right now. If you recently came to believe in Jesus, you are more likely to feel like Mary did. You too have fallen in love, and so the future seems bright because Christ has forgiven your sins and brought you salvation. However, if you have been a disciple for a while and happen to be struggling with some cluster of stubborn problems, you might gravitate a little more toward Job's perspective.

In the immediate aftermath of our decision to exchange agendas with God, we experience conversion euphoria. Sometimes this temporary condition is made more intense by the hyperbole of the person who brought us to Christ. Excited Christians often overplay the triumphs of faith and underplay the disappointments and challenges. They say things such as these: "Give your life to Christ, and he will take care of all your problems." "When you have the Lord on your side, nothing will stand in your way. He will give you all the desires of your heart." Although there is truth in these claims, the truth is much more complex than it sounds to a new believer. Unfortunately, the impression is often left that our faith in Christ will give us a constant experience of total peace, pure joy, and unmitigated delight.

The Magnificat (the common name for Mary's song in Luke 1:46-55) indicates that Mary was experiencing exactly such heightened optimism in the early days of her discipleship. Surely the words of her song are true. The Lord does great things. God shows mercy and strength. There have been clear movements in history when God has scattered the proud, brought down the powerful, lifted up the lowly, filled the hungry, and sent the rich away empty. But there have also been times when the rich have oppressed the poor, the mighty have gotten away with murder, the lowly have been ignored, and the hungry have starved to death. The mere mention of names such as Dachau, Rwanda, Darfur, and Katrina brings aching reminders that God does not always act to save the vulnerable.

I am writing this chapter just a few days after a man went into a one-room Amish schoolhouse in Pennsylvania and killed several young girls before taking his own life. Within just a few hours of this unimaginable tragedy, the Amish community sent representatives to the home of the wife of the man who took their children's lives to offer forgiveness and consolation for her pain. Not a one of those devout believers could have foreseen such an awful challenge to their faith when they took their vows of baptism. When they professed their faith, no doubt they were like Mary and most of us, filled with joyful expectations of the blessings that God was going to bring to their lives. But following Jesus means more than reveling in the great and glorious deeds of God. It also means following Jesus through all sorts of disappointments as well. The truth about following Jesus is that it involves triumph and sorrow, answered prayer and long periods of silence, miracles and misery, but that is not the way it appears in the initial rush of salvation.

Thirteen years separate my third and fourth sons. When I learned that I was going to be a father again after over a decade had passed since my last child was born, I was ecstatic. I thought of the fun that I would have playing with a baby again. I looked forward to watching him learn to crawl, walk, and talk. My mind was flooded with positive images of wrestling with my son on the floor and making him giggle, of waking to magical Christmas mornings as he rushed to see what Santa had left him, of watching cartoons and *Sesame Street* again. Then he was born, and my Pollyanna perspective was given a rude awakening. The baby cried through the night, reintroduced unpleasant odors that had been missing from the house for several years (sending me on frequent runs to the drugstore for diapers), and increased my anxiety about how to keep him out of danger.

Children bring glorious moments to our lives, but they also create new challenges and concerns. The same is true of any life-changing event. I am often frustrated when I do premarital counseling, because the couple, lost in love, can't imagine ever having serious difficulties in their marriage. When I offer help on how to address the problems that marriages encounter, the rapturous couple listens politely but reflects back to me that their love is so unique that it will lift them above the petty issues that distract less enamored men and women. If I am foolish enough to try to pierce this euphoria, I usually get a rather patronizing stare followed by a united testimony that I just don't understand the depth of their love.

Lately I have decided that such responses are okay. If any of us knew all that marriage involved, we probably would run from the altar in panic. If we were fully aware of the gamut of experiences that having a child brings into our lives, we might all pass on the privilege of becoming a parent. Likewise, if faced with the whole range of the costs of discipleship in the infancy of our faith, we might be too intimidated to take the first step. I'm glad that Job wasn't around to counter Mary's conversion euphoria. After all, if we can't feel total exuberance at the announcement of a birth, or during the romantically charged days of new love, or in the initial stages of religious conversion, when will we ever experience such joy? It is right that Mary shouted for joy at the wondrous event that had come upon her. She had encountered the living God, and that God had chosen to bring his only Son into the world through her. Such a holy moment should be celebrated with full-throttled praise.

When we invite Christ into our lives, feel the relief of total forgiveness, sense the new presence of the Holy Spirit, experience the overwhelming love that God has for us, and become filled with gratitude for the eternal life that has been given to us, we too ought to shout and sing and dance for joy. The days after our conversion are not the time to conduct business as usual, play it cool, and describe our new faith in solely rational terms. Like Mary, we ought to let loose the kind of jubilation that is reserved for only the most spectacular events of life—as long as we don't conclude that the infusion of our incredibly merry outlook on life represents the apex of mature discipleship. Because if we make that mistake, then, when we begin to encounter the flip side of following Jesus— the unavoidable letdowns, misunderstandings, and periods of suffering that are part of faithfulness as well—we might falsely conclude that God has abandoned us or that our entire conversion experience was nothing more than an overhyped fantasy.

When I run into a young couple who think that their initial rush of romantic ecstasy represents the pinnacle of true love, I find myself wishing that I could take them to see Bill and Edith. Edith is with the Lord now, but in the last years of her life, her husband, Bill, devoted himself to tending to her. Edith suffered from a combination of ailments that had left her bedridden. Bill had to feed her, clean her, medicate her, comfort her, and respond to her inevitable emergencies. He was exhausted most of the time. And Edith was unable to give Bill much in return. She couldn't go for a walk with him or accompany him on a date to a restaurant. No longer was she able to sit on the couch and hold hands with him as they watched TV. Often she offered Bill a kiss, but the time had long past for her to share in the physical intimacy that fuels young love. Edith's maladies had robbed her of most of the physical beauty that she once had. I think that many people would view Bill's existence with Edith as drudgery. No one would write a song of joy about it.

And yet one day, when I visited the aged couple, Edith, who was going through a particularly difficult phase of her disease, said to her husband, "Bill, do your dance for the preacher." Bill was reluctant, but Edith insisted. She said to me, "Bill does a dance to cheer me up in the evenings. You've got to see it." And then Bill, years past his seventieth birthday, began to move in front of his wife. The performance is hard to describe, but it was somewhere between a bump-and-grind and a hula dance. It was impossible to watch without bursting into laughter, and so I did, and so did Edith and Bill.

The day Edith died, I went to their home. Bill told me that when he knew for sure that his wife had "gone to be with Jesus," as he put it, he began to sing "Joyful, Joyful, We Adore Thee." "But John," Bill wept, "it just didn't sound right. Edith always sang the melody, and I sang tenor. The tenor sounded pitiful all alone." Bill's grief-stricken rendition of the tenor part to "Joyful, Joyful, We Adore Thee" was a far cry from the romantic songs that newlyweds sing, but it was a song of greater love than they could possibly know. That doesn't mean that newlyweds should not sing; it simply means that they should know that the future will be both more wondrous and more terrifying than they can comprehend at the beginning stage of their relationship.

Mary's song was a breathtaking expression of the glad passion of a redeemed soul. All disciples ought to sing such a song when they first experience salvation. But that song does not represent the mature faith that Mary will come to know as her understanding of God deepens. I wish that Mary had written a "Magnificat II" at the end of her life, because I think that it would have been highly instructive for growing disciples. We will see her growth, however, through other incidents in her life. As a model for Christian discipleship, Mary provides us with an inspiring example of the unfettered happiness that rises up in us as we begin our walk with Christ. May we too know such joy even as we acknowledge that what is to come will be both more marvelous and more challenging than our initial euphoria can contain.

## Questions for Reflection

1. What major events have brought a sense of euphoria into your life? In that stage of bliss, how did the future look? What problems did you foresee?

2. When you read Mary's song, do you find yourself saying "Amen" or "Wait a minute, that's not the whole story"? If you were to rewrite Mary's song to make it your own, what changes would you make?

3. When you were converted, what feelings about God, Jesus, your life, and the future did you have? How has your journey of discipleship differed from your initial expectations?

4. Should we encourage people to celebrate their conversion euphoria, or should we confront them with the hard realities of faith right away? What are some of the appropriate ways to celebrate a person's new faith in Christ?

5. How have the hard realities of life diminished or deepened your faith?

# 4

# EVANGELISTIC FERVOR
## The Disciple Shares
## Her Faith

**Matthew 1:18-25**

*Now the birth of Jesus the Messiah took place in this way. When his mother Mary had been engaged to Joseph, but before they lived together, she was found to be with child from the Holy Spirit. Her husband Joseph, being a righteous man and unwilling to expose her to public disgrace, planned to dismiss her quietly. But just when he had resolved to do this, an angel of the Lord appeared to him in a dream and said, "Joseph, son of David, do not be afraid to take Mary as your wife, for the child conceived in her is from the Holy Spirit. She will bear a son, and you are to name him Jesus, for he will save his people from their sins." All this took place to fulfill what had been spoken by the Lord through the prophet: "Look, the virgin shall conceive and bear a son, and they shall name him Emmanuel," which means, "God is with us." When Joseph awoke from sleep, he did as the angel of the Lord commanded him; he took her as his wife, but had no marital relations with her until she had borne a son; and he named him Jesus.*

In his book *The Last Gentleman*, Southern novelist Walker Percy describes a character named Kitty this way: "She was his better half. It would be possible to sit on a bench and eat a peanut butter sandwich with her and say not a word."[1] One might think that Percy was telling of the initial stages of some relationship, the phase in dating in which nerves and unfamiliarity keep us clearing our throats, tapping our fingers, and staring at our shoes while we try desperately to come up with something clever to say. But in fact, the fictional character is depicting a very mature stage in a relationship, one in which words are almost unnecessary because of the ease and intimacy of the love. It is the depth of love that is often depicted by a mature husband and wife, rocking on the front porch, watching the sunset in pure, connected silence.

Some relationships attain that kind of quiet communion after years of loving devotion. But that is not the characteristic of new love. New love is incredibly verbal. One of my teachers once said that new love will get you kicked out of the carpool because the other riders won't stand for your constant chatter about your beloved. When we first fall in love, we want to tell everyone about it. First we gush to our friends and family, but after we wear them out, we will ramble on about the beauty of our true love to total strangers. Sometimes the recipients of our infatuated babbling will receive our words in the spirit in which they are given, smile knowingly, and celebrate with us. Others will find our blabber annoying and will simply walk away while we are in midsentence.

St. John of the Cross said that the same thing happens in the initial stages of discipleship. In the midst of our conversion euphoria, or what he called "love's urgent longings," our feelings are so fresh and powerful that we simply can't keep them to ourselves. We gladly and sometimes proudly share what Christ has done for us with family, friends, and eventually total strangers. Some hear our words and celebrate with us, while others walk away, irritated by our piety and verbosity. But even the threat of a negative response does not chill our enthusiasm. In the "love's urgent longings" stage of discipleship, no challenge seems too great, no call of service too demanding, no act of faith too frightening, no opportunity to witness too intimidating.[2]

Mary's song in Luke 1:46-55, which we looked at in chapter 3, indicates that she was definitely enjoying the "love's urgent longings" stage of discipleship. And following her song of praise, Mary wanted to share what had happened to her with the people of her life. She had conversed directly with the angel Gabriel, and that wasn't even the headline of her gloriously frightening experience. The Holy Spirit had come upon her and conceived the Son of God within her. She was already carrying the baby in her womb, already experiencing the changes that occur to a mother-to-be's body. Her entire life had been redirected through a sacred encounter with God. No doubt, she felt both elated and afraid, about to burst with joy and about to cry with apprehension. It was not the sort of news about which one could keep silent. And yet she also had to know that the response of the people whom she told would be mixed. Some would embrace her and share her joy; others would react with skepticism and alarm, if not complete rejection.

According to the Scriptures, the first person whom Mary told about her encounter with God was her cousin Elizabeth. Luke tells us that immediately after Gabriel left, Mary "set out and went with haste to a Judean town in the hill country, where she entered the house of Zechariah and greeted Elizabeth" (Luke 1:39-40). Elizabeth's response to Mary's good news was total jubilation. Not only did Elizabeth celebrate the news of Mary's new relationship with God, but also the baby in Elizabeth's womb, the future John the Baptist, leapt for joy inside his mother.

Normally, I witness joyful celebration when someone shares the news of his or her conversion. Usually, friends and family, even when they are not that committed to Christ, embrace the new believer and affirm his or her newfound faith. *Usually*, however, is not *always*. During my first pastorate, a sixteen-year-old girl came forward at the close of a worship service and expressed her desire to follow Christ. Her mother followed her down the aisle and smothered her in tears and kisses because she was so happy about her daughter's decision. After the service, I made an appointment to drive out to the family's farm and go over the details of the young girl's upcoming baptism.

When I arrived at the farm, the teenager was in the family's home, but no one else was around. The girl said that her mother was running late and would be home any minute. She added that her father was out in the fields. I had barely begun my explanation of the meaning of baptism when the front door of their home flew open and in walked the girl's father. The burly man was of medium height but of exceptional strength. He entered the living room carrying a pitchfork and asked me in very colorful language about what kind of craziness I was feeding his daughter. He was physically blocking my exit, and since I could not escape, I replied as calmly as I could that I was giving her information concerning her upcoming baptism. It became immediately clear that no one had told him about her conversion. He was not happy. Still holding the pitchfork, he sat down in a chair and listened intently to what I had to say. When I finished, he told me in unmistakable terms to get off his property.

Sometimes people celebrate our professions of faith, and sometimes people disdain our spiritual rebirths. Elizabeth couldn't have been happier, but Mary had another person to tell who had reason to be less enthusiastic. We don't know exactly when Mary told her fiancé, Joseph, about her encounter with God. Luke tells us that she stayed with her cousin Elizabeth for about three months before she returned home. Did Mary break the news to Joseph before she left, or did she take the three months in the Judean countryside to find the spiritual strength and courage to face him with the unexpected announcement? We simply don't know. What we do know is that at some point Mary informed Joseph that she was carrying the Lord's child. The Bible doesn't tell us exactly how she put the revelation. She must have said something like, "Joseph, this is going to be hard for you to believe. Recently the Holy Spirit visited me, and that Spirit conceived a child in me. One day soon I will give birth to the son of God."

Of course, Mary must have done more than simply share the news with Joseph. Matthew tells us that after hearing the news, Joseph had to struggle with whether or not, in light of recent developments, he would go ahead with his plans to become Mary's husband. If Mary had said, "I'm going to give birth to God's son, so obviously the wedding is off," Joseph would not have had to wrestle with what he was going to do. However, Mary didn't simply tell her beloved what had happened to her; she invited him to participate with her in bringing Jesus into this world. Mary must have explained that although Joseph was not needed to conceive the child, he would be tremendously helpful in aiding his delivery, providing for the child's physical needs, and nurturing the child's emotional and spiritual well-being.

Such an invitation required an incredible amount of courage on the part of Mary. Certainly, she knew that the penalty for sexual unfaithfulness during the time of engagement was death. Naturally, Joseph would first assume that the life within her was more likely to have come from an act of sexual impurity than it was to be from the work of the Holy Spirit. She must have wondered whether Joseph would even let her get the words out of her mouth before reacting with anger. When I think of the risks involved in telling Joseph what she had experienced and in inviting him to join with her in presenting Jesus to the world, I wonder why Mary didn't pursue some other option. She could have gone to live with her cousin Elizabeth permanently, found refuge in the home of another family member, or sought protection from another man who would not have been so injured by the news. What gave her the ability to face Joseph with the truth and ask him to continue with his intentions to become her husband and help her raise the child that he knew he had not fathered?

Evangelistic fervor is one name for the dynamic that gave Mary such strength. It is one way of describing the intense need to verbally share our faith in the initial days of our discipleship. Our passion for evangelism spurs us not only to tell others what has happened to us, but also to invite them to participate with us in giving birth to Christ in our generation. Baptists are fond of the biblical phrase "born again." We usually speak of being born again as an experience of spiritual rebirth that provides us with eternal life, and so it does. But that is only part of the story. The phrase also means that God's life or spirit is born in us again. Every believer's life then becomes a semblance of Mary's life. In a very real sense, through each conversion Jesus is being born again and again in every life, every home, every church, and every community. Because this is true, evangelism becomes for us what it was for Mary—an invitation that we issue to others not just to celebrate our conversion, but also to join with us in fleshing out the life of Jesus in our own times. Although we don't know precisely how Mary put this invitation to Joseph, we do know that somehow the evangelistic fervor of her newfound faith gave her the courage to issue it to a man who could have easily reacted with disdain.

The fact of the matter is that Joseph neither celebrated Mary's announcement nor rejected it outright. He struggled with it. Matthew tells us that he wrestled with the decision until he finally decided to call off the engagement as quietly as possible and help Mary to continue her life without him. And that is what Joseph would have done, had the angel of the Lord not visited him in a dream and told him to do otherwise. The angel confirmed to Joseph that Mary's invitation was true and worthy of his acceptance. Specifically, the angel told Joseph that Mary's pregnancy was of the Holy Spirit, and that he was to take Mary as his wife, hold off on having sexual relations with her until after the baby was born, and then name the child Jesus. In other words, Joseph was told by the angel to serve as Jesus' surrogate father. And when Joseph awakened, he did exactly as the angel had directed.

Our eagerness to share our faith and invite others to receive the life of Christ is a wonderful characteristic of the early days of discipleship. The Lord uses this evangelistic fervor to spread the news about Christ's salvation to the people of our lives. Some hear our joyful testimony and immediately assent to following Jesus with us; others hear our invitation and turn away. Some, like Joseph, need to struggle with it awhile. Our privilege is to follow Mary's example and tell our story with an open invitation to others to join us in bringing Christ alive to the people of our world. As we emulate Mary's model of discipleship, it's good to know that the Holy Spirit continues in dialogue with the recipients of our good news long after our words have ceased. Mary didn't convert Joseph; the Spirit of God did. Our sharing won't convert others either. The Spirit will use our story to start the consideration that may ultimately lead to the new birth of the ones with whom we share.

Three Sundays after the teenager whom I mentioned earlier was baptized, I gave the invitation following the sermon, and her father stepped into the aisle and moved forward. When he reached me, he fell to his knees and began to weep. In the conversation that I had with him later that day, the young girl's father told me that it was the witness of his daughter and the evidence of her newfound joy that brought him to faith. Like Joseph, he had to struggle awhile, but then he came to believe.

As the days and months turn into years, and the beginning moments of our conversion recede into the distant past, we may be dismayed at the waning of our evangelistic fervor. When the routine responsibilities of life set in, we often lose the great desire to put our faith into words. This doesn't mean that we don't value our salvation or our relationship with Christ; it simply means that we talk about it with less excitement and urgency. The demands of our job, family, church, and community resume, and we express our faith more by the responsibilities we carry, the ministries we provide, and the services we offer than by what we say. It is a good stage of spiritual maturity, but it is not quite as bright and shiny and verbal. Mary would come to know that stage as well.

However, many disciples rediscover the evangelistic fervor of their faith toward the end of their lives. The years of making money, caring for children, and building a home pass, and they find themselves reconnecting with the more verbal expressions of their faith. Older believers often sign up for mission trips and share their testimonies again with total strangers. Their walk with Christ becomes so meaningful that they simply cannot keep it to themselves, so once again they begin to tell their children, grandchildren, and anyone else who will listen what Jesus has done for them.

My mother is in that time of life right now. Every time I pick her up at the airport, she introduces me to another passenger or airline employee with whom she has shared her faith. One time it was the man who carried her luggage; another time it was a young couple whom she not only introduced to one another, but also made promise to escort each other to church that coming Sunday. When I visit my mother, she never fails to introduce me to a neighbor, store clerk, or cashier with whom she has recently given a witness of the love of Christ. She was not always this way. For years she expressed her deep faith through playing the piano in worship, leading the youth choir, teaching a Sunday school class, caring for my father, raising her children, and building a Christian home. Those were the ways she shared her faith in the middle portion of her life. But now she has rediscovered the verbal side of her faith, and she will talk of it with anyone who will listen.

At the close of Mary's life, she evidently rekindled the verbal nature of her faith as well. If she had not, we never would have received the wondrous stories of the promise and fulfillment of Jesus' birth. She was the only one who knew of those conversations and of the specific events that unfolded the night Jesus was born. Luke could not have received this information from any other source. May we follow her example and share our faith. Share it with those who celebrate with us and with those who treat our testimony with antagonism or struggle until the Spirit gives them the faith to join us in bringing Christ to our own generation.

## Questions for Reflection

1. When have you felt like talking a lot about an experience in your life? What were the various reactions of the people of your life to your chatter?

2. When you were first converted, did you share your experience with friends? Family? Strangers? What were their responses?

3. What are the main ways in which you demonstrate your faith today? What part does verbal witnessing play in your journey right now?

4. Describe someone you know who has come back to a more verbal sharing of his or her faith? What has caused this resurgence in evangelistic fervor? Would you like to experience this resurgence in your own life?

# 5

# THE BIRTHING PROCESS
## The Discipleship Discerns Her True Gift

Luke 2:1-7

*In those days a decree went out from Emperor Augustus that all the world should be registered. This was the first registration and was taken while Quirinius was governor of Syria. All went to their own towns to be registered. Joseph also went from the town of Nazareth in Galilee to Judea, to the city of David called Bethlehem, because he was descended from the house and family of David. He went to be registered with Mary, to whom he was engaged and who was expecting a child. While they were there, the time came for her to deliver her child. And she gave birth to her firstborn son and wrapped him in bands of cloth, and laid him in a manger, because there was no place for them in the inn.*

When Katherine of Aragon gave birth to the son of Henry V on New Year's Day 1511, the celebration of Christmas was extended for two additional weeks. The king and queen sponsored feasts and pageants and jousting tournaments throughout the land. All citizens of the kingdom received extravagant portions of food and drink, and were treated to fine entertainment because the baby was born. Peter the Great gave his citizenry a similar celebration when his son was born in 1700. The grand gala thrown to celebrate the birth included a five-hour fireworks display for the entire kingdom to enjoy. These acts of public generosity pale, however, when compared to what the Sultan of Brunei did to celebrate the birth of his son in the early 1990s. The sultan, who at the time was the world's richest man, built an entire amusement park on par with Disneyland and opened it to all three hundred thousand residents of Brunei for free, all to celebrate the birth of the heir to the throne.

On the day that Jesus was born, Mary had no such luxuries to offer the world. Once she and Joseph arrived in the little village of Bethlehem, they discovered that the only place of hospitable accommodation was filled up with other pilgrims who also had journeyed to their ancestral home. So Mary and Joseph ended up settling in at a stable. Mary gave birth to Jesus in a shelter for animals, wrapped him in the simplest of coverings, and placed him in a feeding trough.

No palace roof or walls sheltered the infant; no majestic tapestries lined the animal stalls. Tradition assumes that some barnyard animals shared the shelter with Jesus, but other than the various beasts of labor and burden that slept in the stable, the birthplace of Jesus was unattended. There was no high priest present, no prestigious government officials. The closest thing to fireworks on that first Christmas was the host of angels that appeared in a distant field, but even that heavenly display was witnessed only by a few peasant shepherds.

The church has always been a little uncomfortable with the stark surroundings of Jesus' birth. Very early on, we wanted to bring the magi into the nativity group photo—never mind that the Bible clearly shows that their visit occurred weeks later, after Mary and Joseph had taken up residency in a home. This seems to reflect the church's desire for a little glitz in the nativity scene. We seem to need for baby Jesus to be surrounded with expensive gifts: gold, frankincense, and myrrh. We've even turned the magi, who were astrologers or sages, into kings. We just can't seem to leave the scene as Luke described it, with just Joseph, Mary, and the baby.

Nevertheless, the birth of Jesus took place in very stark surroundings. Mary didn't have the money to throw a big party to celebrate the birth of her son. She didn't have the material resources to dress him in satin and provide the kind of extravagant birth setting that we seem to want. All that Mary had to offer this world was the baby.

In 2005 several megachurches decided not to hold worship services on Christmas Sunday. Although these congregations had multiple reasons for not opening on Christmas Sunday, the most prominent reason was that it took too many people and too much money to offer the razzmatazz theatrical performances that they felt were necessary to draw a crowd in today's culture. After all, a church can't just put the baby Jesus out there and hope to fill fifteen thousand seats. A church has to surround the baby with lasers and smoke machines, live animals and video screens, orchestras and exquisitely crafted scenery to get people's attention in our society. The baby doesn't seem to be enough for us anymore.

I wonder if Mary had to wrestle with similar urges. She was a new mother, after all, and even the parent of a "normal" baby wants to pass out cigars, send out cute announcements, hang streamers, and string up a bunch of pink or blue balloons to let the neighborhood know that the stork has made a new delivery! Wouldn't Mary have expected at least the first-century equivalent of that? Especially since her son was not just any baby. She had just given birth to the long-awaited Messiah, the one who would sit on David's throne and save the people of Israel! Wouldn't she have been justified in expecting some pomp and circumstance for the newborn king?

However, Luke describes the birth of Jesus in the simplest of terms. "While they were there, the time came for [Mary] to deliver her child. And she gave birth to her firstborn son and wrapped him in bands of cloth, and laid him in a manger, because there was no place for them in the inn." Mary couldn't obtain the fancy accouterments that some felt were needed for the announcement of a royal birth. The only visitors that she had were lowly shepherds, not religious or political dignitaries. Was it then that she began to discern that such extravagances were unnecessary, even diminishing to the true gift that she had to offer the world? She was a novice disciple by many standards, but perhaps even then, Mary may have recognized that humanity had all the superficial flamboyance it could use. Consider the words of the Magnificat, which we looked at in chapter 3, in which she marveled that God had shown favor not to the mighty, but to the poor. Perhaps even as she cradled her newborn baby to her breast, she was coming to understand that this humble beginning was not an oversight or insult. It was profound in its simplicity. I think that even as she lay panting, recovering from her labor, Mary was beginning to discern that the baby was enough.

I'm afraid that many of us who follow Jesus today have never glimpsed Mary's pure insight into discipleship. We have allowed our culture to convince us that the baby is not enough. So we couch the gospel of Jesus Christ in showy presentations that are high on performance quality but low on the stark truth of the baby born to save the world. We have become producers of religious entertainment. Our goal is to show others a good time in the name of Jesus, so we do whatever is necessary to keep them coming back for more. We surround Jesus with all sorts of bells and whistles to keep the attention of those whom we perceive as customers rather than give the only true gift that we have to offer, the gift of the baby.

Several years ago I visited one of our nation's most prominent megachurches. The worship service was carefully planned and moved along like clockwork. It involved live drama, theatrical lighting, a gifted rock band, video displays, and a clever three-point sermon on how to make marriages flourish. Strangely, the name of Jesus was never mentioned. As I left the sanctuary to head for the church's food court, I stopped a young man and asked him why he attended this particular church. He replied without pausing, "Are you kidding? This is the best free show in town." This was not Mary's church. This was a church that believed that the baby was no longer enough.

The *Washington Post* published a fascinating article in the fall of 2005 comparing the ministry of itinerant Pentecostal evangelist Mike Ferree to the ministry of Pentecostal megachurch pastor Joel Osteen.[1] The article describes how Ferree sometimes drives as far as six hundred miles one way to preach to congregations that usually number no more than twenty-five people. The offering collected for the visiting evangelist is seldom more than twenty-five to thirty dollars. Ferree's sermons focus solely on Jesus and the salvation found in his name. Joel Osteen, on the other hand, recently led his congregation, Lakewood Church, to buy the Compaq Center in Houston, Texas, formerly the home of the Houston Rockets basketball team. They renovated the building at a cost of ninety-five million dollars. Osteen's sermons, delivered in that state-of-the-art facility, follow the subject line of the church's slogan: "Discover the champion in you." As many as twenty-eight thousand people flock to hear his positive-thinking sermons each weekend, and millions more witness them on TV. According to the *Washington Post*, the Ferree types have almost disappeared from the face of the earth. Osteen's polish and gleam are what draws a crowd today. Disciples of Jesus all over the nation are concluding that offering just the baby is not enough anymore.

But Mary came to recognize that the baby is all that any disciple has to offer the world. Gabriel did not ask Mary to produce an institution, an event, a show, a program, a political platform, or a religious extravaganza. Mary's unique contribution to the kingdom of God was simply to give birth to the baby. She fulfilled her calling and had to trust that God somehow would take the little boy whom she laid in the feeding trough and change the world.

One of the things that I used to hate about my work as a pastor is now the very thing that I love the most. When I started out in pastoral ministry, I felt inept because it seemed that I had so little to offer people. As a college student, newly ordained to the ministry, I had no power or standing in the community, no reputation or claim to fame, no pearls of wisdom or sage advice from years of experience to give the flock. I had no practical skills to offer; I couldn't fix a broken water pipe or change a spark plug. I had no money to give; I couldn't pay off a mortgage for someone or take care of a medical bill. I couldn't file a lawsuit and win justice for the accused, nor could I pull a few strings and get someone a job. I felt insecure when I responded to people's cries for help. Time after time I entered a hospital room, funeral parlor, nursing home, or a family living room empty-handed. When someone in distress entered my office, I had no toolbox, no medical satchel, no checkbook, no legal brief—nothing to give them to make it all right again. I had nothing.

But now that I've been a disciple for many years, I've come to realize what Mary seemed to know from the very beginning. What I used to see as a liability is actually my only strength. I work without a net. The only thing that I have to offer folks is the baby. If Christ's spirit doesn't heal, I have no other cure. If Christ's love doesn't console, I have no other comfort. If Christ's teachings don't guide, I have no other wisdom. If Christ's strength doesn't liberate, I have no other power. If Christ's love doesn't reconcile, I have no other way to bring people together. If Christ's death and resurrection don't save, I have no other redeeming message. Like Mary, all that I have to offer this world is the baby. That's all that any disciple truly has. But that's all we need.

Several years ago I found myself in a hospital trying to put my life back together after suffering a devastating emotional trauma.

Every morning there was a chapel service to which patients were invited but not required to attend. Looking for all the help I could get, I never missed the service. One morning the young chaplain began his devotion with a prolonged story about a trip he had taken to Guatemala. He was an above-average storyteller, but the details of the excursion seemed to go on and on, and the already unstable congregation was getting increasingly restless. As the chaplain added another side note to his ever-expanding tale, an elderly female patient shouted out, "Just tell us about Jesus! Anybody can tell us about this other stuff."

She was rude, but she was right. Lots of people can spin a good story. Many talented groups can produce plays, musicals, and breathtaking concerts. Numerous organizations can give civic lessons and host political rallies. Only the church can offer Jesus.

As disciples of Christ, we are the ones called to offer the teachings of Jesus, the love of Jesus, the life of Jesus, the vision of Jesus, the service of Jesus, the reign of Jesus, the truth of Jesus, the forgiveness of Jesus, the hope of Jesus, the peace of Jesus. Some may see our gift and size it up as paltry, lackluster, simplistic, unimpressive, and unappealing. Such folks will reject what we have to offer and go in search of life in other places.

Although such rejection undoubtedly will cause us some pain, the answer is not to repackage Jesus in more commercially successful ways. We leave the way of Mary when we add anything to the baby to make him more marketable for our times. For just as surely as some will find the offering of Jesus not enough to sustain their interest and investment, others will find in Christ the answer to their deepest needs. They will discover in the austerity of the manger the very relationship that will give them abundant life.

On one Thanksgiving morning, eighty or so members of the congregation that I pastor gathered to worship our good and generous God. As part of our worship, I served the Lord's Supper. Since the service was being held in our fellowship hall, we administered Communion a little differently. Instead of using our brass trays and plates, we served everyone from a single loaf of bread and from paper cups filled with grape juice. Both the bread and the juice were served on metal trays from the kitchen.

After the service, one of our older members came up to me and complimented the service. Then she added, "At first, though, I was put off by the way you served Communion. You brought me the cup representing Christ's shed blood in an old dirty dishpan. For a moment I was offended. But then, I thought, this is the church. We who follow Jesus are sort of like an old dirty dishpan. The pan is not important. It's only a conveyance. What matters is what the pan contains. The old kitchen tray was made precious solely because it contained the life of Christ. We as disciples are made precious solely because we offer to the world the life of Jesus." The woman understood what Mary understood, what all disciples sooner or later understand. All we have to offer the world is the baby, but praise God, that baby is all the world needs.

Mary discovered this truth right from the beginning. She understood that her calling was to give birth to Jesus in her generation. She knew that her gift to the world was the baby. Unfortunately, Mary's initial clarity would get a little cloudy as she continued to live as a disciple. In the days that followed her beginner's euphoria, Mary would have trouble keeping the focus on Jesus, and sometimes she took center stage herself. The Lord would give her additional experiences until she returned to the mission of her early calling.

Discipleship is not a straight, ascending line. We move back and forth between moments of great clarity about our gift to the world and moments of self-centered arrogance in which we end up promoting our own ideas, egos, and desires. But like Mary, we will have more divinely appointed experiences until we too return to the simple mission to which we have been called. Until we return to offer the world…the baby.

# Questions for Reflection

1. What sort of thoughts do you imagine filled Mary's mind after she gave birth to Jesus? What kind of regrets might she have felt concerning the environment in which Jesus was born?

2. Why do churches often believe that they must produce "religious extravaganzas" for their communities rather than simply tell the story of Christ's birth? What are the pros and cons of these elaborate presentations?

3. When have you felt embarrassed to share Christ with your friends and neighbors? Do we need to make Jesus more commercially viable? Do you ever feel that the story needs a little modernizing in order to be appealing to people in our world today? Why or why not?

4. When has your church become distracted with endeavors other than offering Jesus to your community? What sidetracks your fellowship of disciples? What could bring your church back to focus on offering the baby to your community?

5. When have you wished for something more tangible to offer people in need than simply a spiritual relationship with Christ? How can we offer the love, forgiveness, reconciliation, peace, wisdom, and life of Christ in tangible ways?

6. Mary found great joy in offering the world the baby. What joy have you found in offering Jesus to the people of your world?

# 6

# THE DISCIPLINE OF PONDERING
## The Disciple Learns New Skills

Luke 2:8-20

*In that region there were shepherds living in the fields, keeping watch over their flock by night. Then an angel of the Lord stood before them, and the glory of the Lord shone around them, and they were terrified. But the angel said to them, "Do not be afraid; for see—I am bringing you good news of great joy for all the people: to you is born this day in the city of David a Savior, who is the Messiah, the Lord. This will be a sign for you: you will find a child wrapped in bands of cloth and lying in a manger." And suddenly there was with the angel a multitude of the heavenly host, praising God and saying, "Glory to God in the highest heaven, and on earth peace among those whom he favors!"*

*When the angels had left them and gone into heaven, the shepherds said to one another, "Let us go now to Bethlehem and see this thing that has taken place, which the Lord has made known to us." So they went with haste and found Mary and Joseph, and the child lying in the manger. When they saw this, they made known what had been told them about this child; and all who heard it were amazed at what the shepherds told them. But Mary treasured all these words and pondered them in her heart. The shepherds returned, glorifying and praising God for all they had heard and seen, as it had been told them.*

The church I pastor gathers for a meal on Wednesday nights. The meal gives people a chance to hold the kind of informal conversations that often are impossible on Sunday mornings. Not long ago, I was having such a conversation with a couple of men from our church, when my wife joined us. She waited for us to finish what we were saying and then said, "Did you guys know that they put rose-colored glasses on chickens to keep them from pecking one another to death? My boss told me this at lunch."

Although the two men at my table were too polite to express their true opinions of my wife's announcement, I was not constrained by such social conventions. I said what we were all thinking: "Karen, your boss is messing with you." Karen insisted that it was true, and for a day or two I took advantage of her belief in chickens with spectacles by kidding her about her gullibility. Karen never acquiesced to my disbelief, however, so I searched the Internet for "chickens in eyeglasses."

Much to my surprise, several articles surfaced. It turns out that modern chicken farming has produced some rather feisty chickens—perhaps from the rapid-growth hormones they are given or just from a natural aggression that is exacerbated by crowded chicken coops. (Domestic chickens were originally bred for sport: namely, cockfighting.) In any case, when left unsupervised, the chickens are prone to peck one another, and if they see blood, they keep pecking until they kill their wounded. So sometime in the early 1950s, chicken farmers started attaching tiny red-tinted glasses to each chicken's beak so that the animal couldn't see blood. (Nowadays the chickens wear contact lenses!) If you too have trouble believing this story, I recommend that you go to your local library archives and seek out the *Life* magazine dated April 9, 1956. Grace Kelly is on the cover, and on page 105 you will see chickens wearing glasses. And yes, my wife got several days of "I told you so" mileage from my discovery.

When I learned that people put glasses on chickens, I was amazed. Stuff like that truly amazes me. But that's about all it does. Amazement creates a little stir in our brains. It gives us something to cheer about, laugh about, or share at a dinner party. But amazement doesn't produce lasting change in our lives.

Amazement simply returns in kind the emotion received. It's like Ping-Pong. Someone sends an emotion to us, and we send the same emotion right back. We see amazement at rock concerts. The band runs onto the stage, the lead singer grabs the microphone and yells, "Hello, Boston!" and everyone yells back, "Hello!" The energy of the band and the audience gets looped from one to the other. Amazement is also a frequent occurrence at sporting events. A wide receiver snares a long pass and runs past defenders into the end zone. His heart is pounding, his body is dancing, his voice is shouting. All that energy starts cycling in the stadium through every fan. Adults who normally are fairly reserved leap to their feet and give each other high fives and shout and dance. They give back exactly what they receive. That is amazement.

We often talk for days, sometimes weeks, about what amazes us. "The band sang my favorite song, and fireworks went off, and smoke started rising out of the stage, and everybody started screaming. It was amazing." "The wide receiver bumped the defensive end at the line of scrimmage and then faked to his right and swiveled to his left and blew past him just as he caught the ball. It was amazing." Nothing wrong with amazement; it just doesn't change one's life very much. It's like talking about chickens wearing eyeglasses.

Luke tells us that when Jesus was born to Mary, the angels lit up the sky with songs of praise, and the shepherds were sorely afraid. Another way of translating the Greek word for "afraid" is "scared stiff." But once the angels calmed that fear, what the NRSV translates as terror, the shepherds took that adrenaline rush and went to see what all the heavenly hoopla was about. Scripture doesn't describe their response to what they saw at the stable in Bethlehem, but it seems safe to assume that the initial terror gave way to amazement—in much the same way that a terrifyingly close call on the highway or a heart-in-your-throat roller coaster ride gives way to a sense of amazement or awe. And just as we are bursting with a desire to share that "amazing" experience, the shepherds' amazement was contagious enough to spread to everyone they met. And as they spoke of the incredible things that they had seen, all who heard them were also amazed.

This is precisely the way emotion works. The shepherds deliver the news with awestruck excitement. Virtually every recipient of the amazing story returns the emotion in kind. Did you ever wonder what happened to the shepherds after they encountered the angels and the baby Jesus? We don't know. We never hear about them again. None of them became apostles. They don't resurface at any of Jesus' public teachings. They aren't mentioned at the crucifixion or the resurrection. As far as we know, they saw, they were amazed, and that was it.

The same is presumably true about those who first heard the shepherds' astonishing testimony that night in Bethlehem. Evidently, by the time an adult Jesus began to call disciples, the amazement had worn off. Although we don't know for sure, it's likely that those who received the news with such excitement on the night of Christ's birth had gone on to find other amazing stories and events to celebrate.

Roman Catholic scholar Ronald Rolheiser observes that amazement is usually not a very productive occurrence in the Scriptures. Normally, when people are amazed, Rolheiser says, their connection with the holy is short-lived. When they respond to the word, appearance, or movement of God with amazement, they get quite excited for a short time, and then nothing more develops.[1] They are simply left with an amazing story to tell their friends, like a tale about chickens wearing eyeglasses.

Amazement is one of the primary emotions that disciples experience when they first encounter the presence of God. The disciple is touched by God, and his or her amazement bursts forth in uncontainable gladness. In fact, a disciple in the throes of astonishment can be quite annoying. All that such a believer wants to talk about is what has happened inside, what the mission trip was like, what the sermon inspired, what tears were shed, what love was felt. Such a disciple can be like a roommate who falls in love on a blind date. You're happy for him, but after the tenth cute story of his magical night out with his newfound love, you want to say, "Isn't there anything else you can talk about?" The answer probably is no. He is caught up in amazement.

The powerful emotion locks us into returning to the world exactly what we have received. This can happen with negative as well as positive emotions. We see this demonstrated in the lives of the apostles. When James and John experienced the rejection of a Samaritan village, they asked Jesus if they could return the same kind of treatment to the people of that village that they had received. Specifically, they asked if they could call down fire from heaven upon the discourteous Samaritans. Jesus rebuked their request and taught them to give back something different from the rejection that they had received. On the night of Jesus' arrest, Simon Peter responded to the violent approach of the guards by drawing his sword and cutting off the ear of the high priest's slave. Once again Jesus intervened, scolding Peter for returning to others the same kind of animosity that he had received, and he healed the slave's ear. On both occasions Jesus tried to teach his disciples to respond with something more redemptive than negative amazement.

As followers of Jesus, our calling is to see astonishment for what it is: a quick infusion of energy that is not powerful enough to produce a lasting change. Although we can surely participate in the excitement of the emotion, our calling as disciples is not to follow the example of the shepherds, but rather to emulate the way of Mary. When the shepherds brought their joyous energy to the stable, Mary did not respond with equal levels of praise and exuberance. Luke tells the story this way: "When they [the shepherds] saw this, they made known what had been told them about this child; and all who heard it were amazed at what the shepherds told them" (Luke 2:17-18). Then Luke adds, "But Mary...." The words are highly instructive. Luke has just finished telling us that the shepherds were amazed, and that everyone whom they told about the appearance of the angels and the birth of Jesus shared their excitement—everyone, that is, but Mary. Mary responded differently. Mary pondered what she had heard.

In Hebrew culture, to "ponder" means to hold a feeling inside and carry it for as long as it takes to transform it into something better than what was received. It is essentially the process of spiritual alchemy. In the fourteenth century, pseudoscientists claimed that there was a mysterious stone hidden in the earth—the philosopher's stone—that had the power to speed up the normal process of transformation in the universe. Specifically, they professed that if one rubbed the philosopher's stone against a cheap piece of lead, the stone would change the lead into gold. That process was called alchemy. Pondering is spiritual alchemy. As disciples, we take in emotions, positive and negative, given to us by others and hold them until we can return something better than what we received. We take in lead and ponder it, with the help of the Holy Spirit, until we can give back gold.

Pondering is what Fannie Lou Hamer did in 1963 when she was arrested by corrupt police officers in Winona, Mississippi, and beaten until she passed out. When she came to, she held their hatred in. She did not return it in kind, but rather, by God's grace she pondered the abuse until she was able to give back to her assailants the faith of a gospel song sung from the depths of her soul.[2]

Pondering is what Mamie Till-Mobley did in 1955 after her fourteen-year-old son, Emmett, was killed for simply speaking to (or possibly whistling at) a white woman. Emmett's mother held that pain, anger, and hatred inside until somehow, by the grace of God, it was changed into a productive search for justice. Many years after her son's brutal death, Mamie wrote that she had had a dream in which a voice said, "I have suspended you high above the troubled waters. Keep moving forward. You are headed in the right direction." Awakening from that dream, she said she felt a deep inner peace. She wrote, "I knew that the troubled waters had been hatred and God had guided me over it and away from it. I would not take that plunge, and I was so thankful…I never felt any hatred for Bryant and Milam [the men who had killed her son]. And I did not want them to be executed. I wanted justice.… I want it still."[3]

And pondering is what Corrie ten Boom did in the years following World War II. She held deep inside the pain, anger, and hatred that were dished out to her and her sister in the women's extermination camp in Ravensbrück, Germany. She prayed over it and sought God's help in transforming it into something far better than what she had received. Long after the war ended, Corrie gave her testimony of God's salvation at a church in Munich, Germany. As she left the church following her presentation, a man approached her whom she immediately recognized as one of her jailers at Ravensbrück. He said with great exuberance, "How grateful I am for your message, Fräulein. To think that, as you say, Jesus has washed all my sins away." Then he held out his hand.

Corrie ten Boom wrote in her memoir that she tried to raise her hand to his but could not. She felt an intense desire for revenge. So she asked Christ to help her. She said that she had to pray three times before she could muster the strength to stretch out her hand to her former tormentor. But as she did, she felt an unexplainable love for this man who had given her unbearable pain.[4] That is what it means to ponder.

The first dozen or so times I asked my wife to marry me, I got the same disturbing response. She simply said, "We'll see." Back then, I was confused by her noncommittal answer, but now I understand the importance of what she was saying. "We'll see" are the words of a ponderer. She meant, "John, I share your excitement over this newfound love, but I'm not going to answer in the passing emotion of amazement. I'm going to ponder this, hold it inside awhile. If the lead of excitement is transformed into the gold of love, I'll say yes. Until then, we'll see." My wife knew that no life-changing decision is made in the midst of amazement. Enduring relationships are born from the hearts of ponderers— people who take in the intense, fleeting energies of life and hold them until they become something far more powerful than the emotion given to them.

I believe that pondering is the characteristic that most identifies people as followers of Jesus, for our Lord was the consummate ponderer. From the night of his birth, when there was no room for him in the inn, to the day of his crucifixion, when he took in all the hatred of the world and gave back love, Jesus lived his life receiving the lead of this world and pondering it until he could give back gold.

I don't know what gave Mary the ability to ponder when the rest of the disciples found it such a difficult skill to learn. Mary took in the experiences surrounding Jesus' birth and held them in silence. She felt no compulsion to comment on them, explain them, or defend them. Instead, she observed all that happened around her—the excitement, the mystery, the uncertainty, the adoration—and held it all deep within, giving the Spirit time to change it into a deep and genuine faith.

Quite possibly, it was her state of pregnancy followed by her nursing responsibilities that gave Mary time to sit and ponder all that was unfolding in her life. New mothers often speak about the deeply spiritual experiences that they have as they give nurture to the miracle of new life. Mary, no doubt, experienced similar mysteries. And as she did, she let the Spirit transform the superficial emotions of amazement into the sturdy foundations of sincere devotion. Unlike the shepherds, Mary followed Jesus all the way to the cross.

We too are called to times of silent reflection concerning the mysteries of our lives. Mary can teach us the value of holding some experiences, thoughts, questions, and struggles within in order to give the Spirit time to transform passing emotions into more mature gifts of God. When we feel compelled to talk too soon, respond too quickly, formulate immediate answers and explanations for the spiritual encounters of our lives, we often simply return to the world the same emotion, treatment, or perspective that we have received. Seldom is that the response of mature discipleship.

The pondering that Mary did in the immediate aftermath of the birth of Jesus stored up wisdom for the challenges that awaited her. When she drew upon that preserved wisdom, Mary exhibited a rich and highly developed sense of spiritual awareness. When she ignored what she had learned in her moments of deep reflection, she reverted to shallow reactions to the frustrations of her journey with Christ. Her journey of discipleship was still to have many ups and downs ahead. However, through the experience of pondering, the Lord added a new discipline to Mary's repertoire that enabled her to respond to the glory and pain of her life with a depth rarely seen. May we too learn the discipline of pondering.

## Questions for Reflection

1. Think of something that has amazed you in the past. Has this amazing observation had any long-term effect on your life?

2. When have you felt excitement over an encounter with God? Did that excitement last? Why or why not?

3. How did Mary's response to the birth of Jesus differ from the response of the shepherds? Why did she have the ability to ponder these events when so many of her contemporaries reacted impulsively?

4. Do you know any ponderers? How do they respond to major emotional events in their lives? Can you think of any historical examples of people who returned to the world something better than the treatment they received?

5. Are you more likely to react quickly to a powerful event in your life, or are you more likely to spend time reflecting on the occurrence before responding? When you have reacted swiftly to emotional episodes in your life, were you generally proud or regretful of your behavior?

6. Have you found silence, music, nature, art, darkness, solitude, houses of worship, companionship, or guidance to be most helpful when you need to ponder?

7. What emotions or experiences do you need the Spirit to perform spiritual alchemy on? Have you received treatment that you are tempted to return in kind? What do you need to do to allow the Spirit to turn that lead into gold?

*Silent Reflection*

# 7

# THE WHOLE PICTURE
## The Disciple Learns of Suffering

Luke 2:21-35

*After eight days had passed, it was time to circumcise the child;
and he was called Jesus, the name given by the angel before he
was conceived in the womb.*

*When the time came for their purification according to the law
of Moses, they brought him up to Jerusalem to present him to
the Lord (as it is written in the law of the Lord, "Every firstborn
male shall be designated as holy to the Lord"), and they offered
a sacrifice according to what is stated in the law of the Lord, "a
pair of turtledoves or two young pigeons."*

*Now there was a man in Jerusalem whose name was Simeon;
this man was righteous and devout, looking forward to the consolation of Israel, and the Holy Spirit rested on him. It had been
revealed to him by the Holy Spirit that he would not see death
before he had seen the Lord's Messiah. Guided by the Spirit,
Simeon came into the temple; and when the parents brought in the
child Jesus, to do for him what was customary under the law,
Simeon took him in his arms and praised God, saying, "Master,
now you are dismissing your servant in peace, according to your
word; for my eyes have seen your salvation, which you have*

*prepared in the presence of all peoples, a light for revelation to the Gentiles and for glory to your people Israel."*

*And the child's father and mother were amazed at what was being said about him. Then Simeon blessed them and said to his mother Mary, "This child is destined for the falling and the rising of many in Israel, and to be a sign that will be opposed so that the inner thoughts of many will be revealed—and a sword will pierce your own soul too."*

Across the street and down the block from my boyhood home lived a large family. The parents had five children when they conceived again and produced twins. About twice a year the mother of this group called my mother and officially invited my little brother and me to their home for what she always referred to as a "gala affair." My younger brother and I dreaded these invitations like we dreaded turnip greens on the supper table. My mother never inquired as to whether we wanted to attend; she simply accepted the invitation on our behalf and announced that we had a nice party to attend. Had my mother ever attended one of these "gala affairs," she would have known better.

When the horrid day of the party arrived, my brother and I put on our Sunday school clothing and were sent off to "have fun." The mother of the brood always met us at the front door and escorted us to the backyard, where there was a card table covered in a pink tablecloth surrounded by kitchen chairs on which we were invited to sit. Once we were in place, the youngest squadron of her children was set free to pour out upon the lawn. I say "lawn," but there were so many tricycles and pogo sticks, hula-hoops and wagons, bicycles and croquet mallets strewn about that anything approximating grass had been stomped out long ago. The youngest siblings circled around my brother and me. They always seemed to have colds, and they filled the air with snorts and sneezes, coughs and wheezes. They yelled and screamed and threw dust in the air and pulled on our Sunday clothes while asking us why we dressed up.

Then the daughter nearest our age made her entrance. Dressed like a character from a Tennessee Williams play, she presented herself in formal attire and sat between my brother and me. Her mother followed her outside and placed a pitcher of cherry Kool-Aid and a plate of vanilla wafers on the table. When the cookies were exposed, the younger kids crashed into the table like piranhas on a wounded calf and devoured all the wafers before my brother and I could taste a morsel. During the battle for cookies, they usually tipped over the Kool-Aid, spilling the sticky liquid onto our Sunday best.

The girl our age hollered at her siblings to act civilized, which they ignored and started yanking on her party dress and chanting stuff about her having two boyfriends, who turned out to be my brother and me. Screams, laughter, teasing, and repulsive bathroom humor ensued from the obnoxious children. And then the mother, who by that point was sprawled out on a reclining lawn chair, rather wistfully said, "Now, isn't this nice?" I was just a boy, forbidden from challenging the insane comments of adults. But I always wanted to scream, "No, this is not nice. This is in no way nice. Your children are wild. Your daughter is troubled. There is danger here. This is not a gala affair. It is something much closer to social work intervention time."

Sometimes I think that we followers of Christ are as deluded as my boyhood neighbor. We read the Bible, a holy book filled with stories of creation and destruction, liberation and slavery, wondrous births and ghastly infanticide, happy unions and devastating affairs, blessings and curses, stubborn hope and dark despair, angels and demons, rescues and imprisonments, miraculous protections and wholesale massacres, shining stars and blood-filled moons, nail-pierced hands and resurrected bodies, and say, "Isn't this nice?" God must feel like screaming, "This is not nice. This is nowhere near nice. This is wild and dangerous. This is what it cost to love in a world bent on destruction.

Take the rose-colored glasses off and see it for what it is. Yes, there is glorious triumph here, but it comes at an awful price. It is not nice."

Mary and Joseph brought Jesus to the temple in Jerusalem thirty-three days after his birth. They did so to fulfill the Jewish law that required parents to make an offering of five shekels for their first-born son and to offer sacrifices to purify the mother after child-birth. While Mary, Joseph, and Jesus were in the temple, the Spirit led an old saint by the name of Simeon to enter the house of worship. Luke tells us that Simeon was looking forward to seeing the child who would bring consolation to Israel. When Simeon saw Jesus, he recognized him to be the fulfillment of the ancient messianic promise. The old man took Jesus into his arms, praised God, and thanked the Lord for allowing him the opportunity to see the Messiah. Simeon told God in that moment of joy that he could now die in peace, for he had seen the one who would bring salvation to the world, revelation to the Gentiles, and glory to Israel.

Consolation, salvation, peace, light, revelation, glory—doesn't that sound nice? The whole scene and accompanying script would make a beautiful Christmas card. Many of us come to believe in Christ because of the nice things we hear about him. We learn that he offers forgiveness, liberation, salvation, eternal life, redemption, hope, joy, peace, and love. It sounds great, so we sign up, invite the Savior in, and celebrate our sweet relation-ship with Jesus.

Luke tells us that when Mary heard Simeon's first pronounce-ment, she and Joseph were amazed. Remember the danger with being amazed. It provides a shot of spiritual adrenalin for a short period of time, but it rarely produces a lasting change. Mary was bowled over by all the nice things that Simeon had to say about her son. But astonishment is not enough to make a disciple of Jesus Christ; something more is needed. And Mary, as a model of what it means to be a follower of Jesus, was about to learn what more was required. Simeon spoke again, and this time his words were not so appealing. He turned to Mary (notice how Luke specifies that the old saint is addressing these words to her) and said, "This child is destined for the falling and rising of many in Israel, and to be a sign that will be opposed so that the inner thoughts of many will be revealed—and a sword will pierce your own soul too." This is not nice. This is not nice at all.

Imagine how you'd feel if you brought your newborn for dedication at church and something like this happened to you. After some sweet hymns were sung and a precious prayer was offered and you were presented with a cute baby book and a pretty rose, the pastor stepped back to the microphone and said, "I have received a prophecy concerning this child." Then, after some awkward throat clearing, the pastor said, "This boy is destined to wreck his car at the age of seventeen and alter every family member's life forever," or "This girl is destined to run off at the age of fifteen with a man old enough to be her father," or "This son is destined to give his life fighting in a war at the age of nineteen." I expect that you would protest and say, "That's not nice. You ruined our baby dedication."

If it was niceties that Mary expected, then Simeon ruined the whole event. But Simeon, as a mouthpiece for God, could not allow Mary to walk away from the dedication of her baby thinking only happy thoughts, as if following Jesus was going to be like attending a lovely tea party in the neighbor's backyard. He wanted Mary to know that it was going to be more ominous than that. There would be wondrous joy, but it would come only through wildness, suffering, and danger. The child would be opposed by enormous evil, and the followers of the child would be pierced by terrible pain.

Simeon captured the awful essence of his prophecy when he promised, "This child is destined for the falling and rising of many in Israel." Many biblical interpreters claim that this phrase comes as both a warning to those who reject Christ and a comforting promise to those who follow the Lord. They say that those who turn away from Christ's offer of salvation will fall to their spiritual doom, and those who embrace Christ will rise to their spiritual triumph.

Yet there is at least one other way to interpret this phrase. New Testament scholar G. B. Caird writes in his commentary that Simeon is telling Mary that all who follow Jesus will experience a falling and rising. The falling is not just for those who refuse to believe in Jesus, nor is the rising reserved for a few the souls who find faith in Christ. Instead, Caird argues, both the falling and the rising are experienced by every disciple.[1] When we do the work of Christ and receive affirmation, blessing, and support, we sense a rising of our spirit. However, when that same Christian love is met with persecution, criticism, and disdain, we suffer the pain that can bring us down to the depths spiritually.

Of course, we who follow Jesus would like to believe that Caird is wrong. We would like to convince ourselves that suffering is reserved for those who are antagonistic to the cause of Christ, while blessed peace is all that those of us who love Christ will ever know. However, the teaching of Scripture, as well as our life experience, defies such false assurance.

A few years ago a woman in great distress came to see me. She was a recent immigrant to this country, and nothing had gone well since she arrived. Her marriage was falling apart, she was barely surviving financially, and she was sinking into bitterness. The woman knew nothing about the Bible, so I gave her one and told her to look through it and bring it back to me with any questions she might have. I assured her that Christ would help her begin to put her life back together, and that I, as one of Christ's representatives, would help her in any way I could. I then said a prayer with her, and she went home.

Less than a week later, she returned. Before I could say anything to her, she returned the Bible and said, "I don't want anything to do with this book or the people who believe in it." When I asked why, she replied, "Because everyone in it suffers. Why would I want a religion in which everybody suffers?"

Few if any of us want that. Not long ago my eight-year-old son and six-year-old daughter bugged their mother and me incessantly to take them to the movie version of C. S. Lewis's *The Lion, the Witch, and the Wardrobe*. We had some reservations that the allegory based on the life, death, and resurrection of Jesus Christ might be too emotional for my daughter, but after discussing the matter with some friends, we agreed she could go. We prepared her by telling her that Aslan, the lion character who represented Christ, was going to be killed in the movie, and that would no doubt be sad. But we added, "He will come back to life, just like Jesus rose again from the grave on Easter." Our daughter nodded that she understood, and off we went to the cinema complex.

Sure enough, the movie version was very dramatic. Aslan the lion was huge, wise, and fierce. At one point he roared menacingly and stomped the earth in a threatening fashion. As Aslan turned away to carry out the rest of his mission, one disciple turned to another and said, "Well, after all, he is a lion, and he is not a tame one." My daughter was able to take these vivid presentations of the undomesticated lion. But when the evil spirits began to harm the lion, when they tied him up, shaved his beard, and began to inflict pain upon him, she turned to her mother and tearfully said, "I want to go to another movie now."

Mary might have had similar feelings as she listened to Simeon expose her to the suffering side of loving Jesus. Possibly she thought, "No one told me that there would be pain involved in this. No one mentioned a sword piercing me or trouble coming to the baby. I'd like to go to another mission now." But escaping the suffering associated with loving Jesus was not her prerogative. According to the Gospel of Matthew, after Jesus was born, King Herod ordered the slaying of all the boys in the region of

Bethlehem who were two years of age or younger. In response to that atrocity, Mary had to take her son and flee with her husband, Joseph, to Egypt. Matthew further reports that even after the mad king died, Mary and Joseph were too afraid to return to the place of Jesus' birth. Instead, they took the boy to Nazareth, where they felt that he would be safe from the violent actions of those in power.

Simeon was right. Almost from the beginning of her son's days, Mary had to grapple with the suffering involved in loving Jesus. And as Jesus grew, Mary had to face even more painful moments, culminating in the crucifixion of her blessed son. Until her encounter with Simeon, she was told nothing but positive elements concerning Jesus' life. But the stark truth was that some of the days ahead would bring more sorrow into Mary's life than she had ever known or could have imagined. As difficult as it must have been for Mary to hear, Simeon did her a great service by helping to prepare her for the painful aspects of discipleship.

As followers of Jesus, we too must be prepared to experience suffering. Pain is not reserved for those who disobey the Lord. It is part of the life of the faithful follower as well. Sometimes we will be mistreated because we love Jesus. There will be people who dislike us and possibly even persecute us because we follow Christ, especially when we choose to speak out against injustice that benefits some people or call attention to behaviors that transgress the teachings of Jesus. Sometimes, even when we are trying to help someone in need, we might receive anger or scorn in response from the very people we are trying to assist. Jesus was treated the same way.

We will also suffer because Christ will make our hearts tender toward the needs of others. Disciples of Jesus lose the ability to ignore the plight of the hungry, homeless, oppressed, lonely, and abused people of this world. When we are confronted with their suffering, we feel it too. Our sorrow also becomes intense when we watch others ignore or reject the love of Christ. To watch a loved one go deeper into destructive habits even as Christ reaches out with love and forgiveness is intensely painful. When we pray for a loved one to see the love that Christ had demonstrated for him or her, and then watch as this person blindly stumbles on into despair, it grieves us enormously. Our pain is heightened also when we watch the immensity of the suffering that people inflict on one another through war, violent crimes, domestic abuse, and other acts of inhumanity. As we watch a world for which Christ died seem bent on destroying itself, we suffer.

Wouldn't it be nice if all were joy and comfort in the way of discipleship? But that is not reality. As followers of Jesus, we must emulate Mary in preparing our hearts for the suffering that is part and parcel of loving Jesus. Like Mary, we cannot exchange this calling for another mission. We cannot go to another movie. The way of suffering is the way God chooses to redeem this world.

## Questions for Reflection

1. What sort of emotions did Mary feel when she heard Simeon thank God that he had seen the Messiah? How did those emotions change when Mary heard the same prophet speak of the pain that Jesus would face and bring to her?

2. Who was most instrumental in helping you become a Christian? In preparing you for discipleship, did that person talk about the good things that Christ would bring to your life? Did that person also try to prepare you for the suffering that would follow?

3. What would you say to those who believe that suffering is reserved for the unrepentant, while people of true faith are protected from such pain?

4. When did you first understand that suffering was part of faithful discipleship?

5. How have you suffered for the cause of Christ? What helps prepare you for the suffering that may yet occur in your journey of discipleship?

# 8

# LOSING JESUS
## The Disciple
## Regresses

### Luke 2:41-50

*Now every year his parents went to Jerusalem for the festival of the Passover. And when he was twelve years old, they went up as usual for the festival. When the festival was ended and they started to return, the boy Jesus stayed behind in Jerusalem, but his parents did not know it. Assuming that he was in the group of travelers, they went a day's journey. Then they started to look for him among their relatives and friends. When they did not find him, they returned to Jerusalem to search for him. After three days they found him in the temple, sitting among the teachers, listening to them and asking them questions. And all who heard him were amazed at his understanding and his answers. When his parents saw him they were astonished; and his mother said to him, "Child, why have you treated us like this? Look, your father and I have been searching for you in great anxiety." He said to them, "Why were you searching for me? Did you not know that I must be in my Father's house?" But they did not understand what he said to them.*

I was a grader in seminary for a church history professor. Just before Thanksgiving break one year, the professor gave a long, comprehensive final. The test was to count for one-third of each student's grade. As I was leaving to spend the holiday with my grandparents, the instructor gave 112 exams to me and asked me to grade them while I was away. I carefully placed the valuable cargo in a sturdy cardboard box. I put the box on the floorboard in the backseat of my car and drove to Jena, Louisiana, where my grandparents lived. The air conditioner in my Volkswagen Rabbit had worn out, so, since it was a warm, sunny day, I rolled the windows down about a third of the way and journeyed to my destination in relative comfort.

When I arrived at my grandparents' home, I grabbed my suitcase and went in to greet them. Thanksgiving dinner was ready, so we ate right away. As we feasted, we commented on the cloudburst that had begun to come down on the roof of their home. It was well after dessert before I remembered the exams on the floorboard of my car. I ran out and retrieved them. They were soaked. Feverishly, I carefully separated the pages of the blue books, only to find that I couldn't read a single word. The exams completed in pencil were so faint that I couldn't see the answers. The exams done in pen were illegible because the ink had bled into the paper. On my way to Thanksgiving dinner, the tests had great value, but after the rain they lost their content. And with that loss, the tests became virtually worthless.

Over the years I have read many commentaries on Jesus' visit to Jerusalem as a twelve-year-old boy. Every one of them has exonerated Mary and Joseph for losing their son. Although I no longer remember who wrote it, the best explanation that I found gave a clear rationale for their parental oversight. The key to understanding the misplacement of Jesus, the author said, is his age. The people of Nazareth would have traveled together on the journey to Jerusalem for the Passover. However, the scholar continued, the men, women, and children would not have walked in one group. Instead, the men would have clumped together so they could discuss whatever it was that men liked to talk about back then. The women likewise would have coalesced to share whatever was on their minds. As is true of many cultures, the children would have traveled with their mothers. So, on his way to Jerusalem, Jesus, still being seen as a child, would have been with Mary. However, after attending the Passover for the first time as a twelve-year-old, Jesus would have been considered a *bar mitzvah*, or "son of the law," and in the eyes of the law, a man, responsible for his own devotion to God. As a man, Jesus would no longer be expected to journey with the women and children, but rather would have been required to walk in the company of the other men.

Mary, the commentator theorized, being more attuned to the developmental stages of her son, would therefore have assumed that Jesus was with his father and the other men on their trek back home. Joseph, according to the scholar, being less aware of the rites of passage of his son, would have assumed that Jesus was walking home with the women and children. Not until nightfall, when the families began to reunite and bed down for sleep, would Joseph have thought to ask Mary, "Where is Jesus?" She would have replied, "I thought he was with you." When both parents realized that they had made false assumptions about their twelve-year-old's whereabouts, they would have frantically retraced their steps to find their missing son, as the Scripture indicates. From that scholar's perspective, the losing of Jesus was due simply to miscommunication on the part of the parents. It could have happened to anybody.

Although this is not a bad interpretation of the passage, it works against our getting the full meaning of the text. Most of us who are parents have lost a child for a few heart-wrenching moments at a store or event. So it is easy for us to identify with Joseph and Mary and let them off the hook. But I don't think that Luke wants us to be so understanding. Instead, I believe that

Luke wants us to read this story and say to ourselves, "How could parents leave a big city like Jerusalem without being sure that their twelve-year-old son was with them? Twelve-year-olds are especially susceptible to danger and temptation. Of all age groups, twelve-year-olds in particular need careful supervision from their parents. Shouldn't they have talked with Jesus before launching on such a trip and made sure that they knew where he would be on the journey? Don't decent parents at least make eye contact with all their children before they begin a sixty-mile walk home? What were these folks thinking?"

Rather than absolve the parents of any culpability for losing their son, I think that Luke wants us to feel at least a little outrage at their behavior. We need to be somewhat appalled at their negligence in order to properly respond to the next part of the story, when Luke puts the spotlight on Mary. Luke relates that when Jesus' parents finally checked the temple to see if their son might be there, it was Mary who spoke in exasperation. She said, "Child, why have you treated us like this? Your father and I have been searching for you in great anxiety."

Hold on a minute! Who was responsible for whom? Mary asked Jesus, "Child [note the language here; contrary to the interpretation discussed above, Mary still saw Jesus as a child], why have you treated us like this?" If Jesus was a child, then he did what children do. They get distracted, they follow after what interests them, and they wander off. It is the parents' job to keep track of the child. I believe that Luke wants us to shake our heads at Mary and think, "Jesus should be asking you, 'Why did you treat me like this? Why did you go off without me?'"

Then Luke gives Jesus' perspective on his mother's awareness. He reports that Jesus said to his mother, "Why were you searching for me? Did you not know that I must be in my Father's house [or, 'doing my Father's business']?" Since we don't have an audio or video recording of this interaction between son and mother, we can't be positive about the tone with which Jesus spoke. To my ears, Jesus seemed to be expressing some incredulity with his mother's obliviousness about his location. At the very least, we can say that Jesus did not excuse his mother's oversight. Jesus did not say, "That's all right, Mother, anybody could lose their son in a city this big. I know I'm in a transitional stage right now between childhood and adulthood, and it was natural for you to assume that I was traveling with Father. I can understand why, when you noticed that I wasn't traveling with you, you looked in a thousand other places before searching the temple grounds. I know that I'm a little different and hard to figure out." No, Luke tells us that Jesus was unnerved by the fact that his own mother didn't know to look for him in the temple. Luke wants us to be somewhat unsettled by this as well. I believe that Luke also wants us to ask, "How could Mary, of all people, be so out of touch with her son's desires, calling, and identity that she would look everywhere else in town before going to the one place where he was most likely to be found?"

Mary lost her son, and for three days she didn't know where to find him. We might feel better by keeping the focus on Mary, but that is not Luke's purpose in telling this story. Instead, the writer wants us to turn the light of Scripture on our own behavior and ask, "How can we, the disciples of Jesus Christ, of all people, lose Jesus? And why, when we realize that we've lost him, don't we immediately know that we can find him when we return to do his Father's business?"

Mary journeyed for a day before realizing that she had lost Jesus. Sometimes we modern disciples go on for years without noticing that we've lost him. Why? We substitute something else in his place. And in most cases we become much more faithful to the substitute than we ever were to Jesus. That substitute can be, among other things, a denomination, church, political perspective, theological viewpoint, liturgical tradition, or pastor. Simone Weil observes that there are servants in some cultures who are so faithful to their masters that they will wait at the master's door until they die of hunger if their master does not come and dismiss them.[1] Weil applauds the faithfulness of such folks, but I don't. Faithfulness, in and of itself, is not necessarily a commendable virtue. Disciples are not laudable for being faithful to an agenda if that agenda has lost Jesus.

Sometimes we can become so dedicated to our perspective on what music should be played in worship, who should get the credit for vacation Bible school, or what political opinion our pastor should hold that we end up breaking off relationships with those in the church who hold viewpoints that oppose ours. Out of a compulsion to stay faithful to our own perspective, we become unfaithful to Jesus' directive to love one another. Frequently, congregations use all their energy wrangling over these less important matters and have no resources left over to help the poor, evangelize the lost, reconcile the estranged, comfort the brokenhearted, take prophetic positions of justice, or do any of the other things that Jesus commanded us to do. In such cases, other issues replace Jesus, and we become so all-consumed with them that we don't even notice that he is temporarily lost from the life of the church.

We can lose Jesus in our personal lives as well. St. Augustine experienced this during a period in his life when other issues took the place that Jesus once held in his passions. He said that he had to pull himself together from "the scattered fragments into which I was broken and dissipated during all that time when, being turned away from you, the one, I lost myself in the distractions of the many."[2] When I get so bogged down in the mechanics of operating a church, the responsibilities of maintaining a home, the stresses of paying bills, the banalities of what is shown on TV, and the constant demands of my children's schedules that I no longer keep the spirit of Christ at the center of my life, I become miserable. I don't want to spend my life focusing on petty problems, hollow entertainment, and inconsequential issues. Like Mary, when I realize that I've let the relatively minor details of the journey distract me from keeping my eyes on Jesus, I have an almost frantic desire to find him again.

So what do we do when we realize that we've lost Jesus? When I realized that I had lost the content of those exams, I did the only thing I could think of doing. I blanketed my grandmother's guest bedroom with bath towels. Then I covered the bath towels with soggy exams. I opened the curtains and the blinds and let the sunshine pour in upon them, and then I waited for a day. And as they dried out, a miracle occurred. The dry paper reabsorbed the bleeding ink of the exams done in pen, and I could read them clearly again. As the water in the exams done in pencil evaporated, the paper reflected the graphite more clearly, and I could make out those answers as well. Within two days, I could once again read every test. With the content restored, the blue books were once again of great value.

When we realize that we've temporarily lost Jesus, we must find a way to restore him, the valuable content of our spiritual journey, to his rightful place. The founding spirit of the singing group Sweet Honey in the Rock, Bernice Johnson Reagon, gives this advice: "If, in moving through your life, you find yourself lost, go back to the last place where you knew who you were, and what you were doing, and start from there."[3] Like Mary, we have to journey back to the last place where we had Jesus in sight. Mary learned from Jesus that the place to reconnect with him is always the same. We restore Jesus to the center of our lives when we return to doing the Father's business. That is where Jesus is always to be found, and that is where disciples should be found as well. By returning to the house of worship to hear again the words of God, and then by obeying those words through forgiving someone who has hurt us badly; teaching our children the ways of Christ; rebuilding our marriage on the love of Christ, sharing our resources with those who are in need; speaking out against racism, violence, and the evils of our age; befriending someone who is feeling abandoned; loving someone who is really hard to love; or sharing our faith with a friend who has lost the way, we always rediscover Jesus.

Luke is telling us that of all people, Mary should not have lost Jesus. She began her walk of discipleship with great resolve and clarity. She learned how to ponder the truth of Christ until amazement had been transformed into true faith. The mother of Jesus had even begun to comprehend the place of suffering in her walk of faith. But then she regressed. Somehow, over the passage of twelve years, she became distracted and lost sight of the true nature of the one she knew to be the Savior of the world.

Of all people, the disciples of Jesus Christ should not lose Jesus. But we do. As the years go by, other loyalties and priorities and attractions usurp the content of our faith, and we actually lose sight of Jesus. Something else substitutes for dedication to Christ, and we become so rigidly committed to the substitute that we don't even look for Jesus anymore.

The only way to recenter ourselves on Jesus is to do what Mary did. When I say that Mary is a model for Christian discipleship, I don't mean that everything that she did is to be emulated. I mean that we can learn from everything that she experienced in her efforts to understand and follow Jesus. Up until this visit to Jerusalem, Mary had made significant progress in her growth as a disciple. In fact, her movement toward maturity had been relatively steady. But novice disciples don't transform into saints by advancing along perfectly ascending lines. The best ones, like Mary, soar to great heights of spiritual insight but also fall in the midst of their own human frailties. The writers of the Gospels are intent on telling the whole story, not the edited, sanitized version, of the ups and downs involved in following Jesus.

However, Mary learned from her mistakes, and as we will see in the next chapter, she put Jesus back front and center in her life. May we too recommit ourselves to walking with Jesus as together we do our Father's business.

# Questions for Reflection

1. Have you ever temporarily lost a child who was under your supervision? What were your thoughts and feelings? What did you do?

2. What is your opinion of Mary and Joseph's inability to keep track of Jesus on their way home from Jerusalem? What do you think of Mary's words to Jesus when she finds him? What do you think of his response?

3. What are some of the signs that a church has lost its focus on Jesus? To what or whom do churches dedicate themselves when they lose sight of Jesus? How long does it take a church to realize that it has lost Jesus from the center of its life?

4. Have you ever felt that you have temporarily lost Jesus in your journey of discipleship? If so, what helped you realize that he was missing? What did you do?

5. What does it mean to recommit to doing the Father's business? How can that help us rediscover Jesus?

6. Do you need to do anything to restore Jesus to the center of your life? If so, what?

# 9

# PLACING JESUS FRONT AND CENTER
## The Disciple Refocuses

### John 2:1-12

*On the third day there was a wedding in Cana of Galilee, and the mother of Jesus was there. Jesus and his disciples had also been invited to the wedding. When the wine gave out, the mother of Jesus said to him, "They have no wine." And Jesus said to her, "Woman, what concern is that to you and to me? My hour has not yet come." His mother said to the servants, "Do whatever he tells you." Now standing there were six stone water jars for the Jewish rites of purification, each holding twenty or thirty gallons. Jesus said to them, "Fill the jars with water." And they filled them up to the brim. He said to them, "Now draw some out, and take it to the chief steward." So they took it. When the steward tasted the water that had become wine, and did not know where it came from (though the servants who had drawn the water knew), the steward called the bridegroom and said to him, "Everyone serves the good wine first, and then the inferior wine after the guests have become drunk. But you have kept the good wine until now." Jesus did this, the first of his signs, in Cana of Galilee, and revealed his glory; and his disciples believed in him. After this he went down to Capernaum with his mother, his brothers, and his disciples; and they remained there a few days.*

When Katie Holmes married Tom Cruise in November 2006, the church was packed with celebrities from the worlds of music, cinema, stage, and politics. But that guest list pales when compared to the record of those in attendance at the wedding at Cana. The apostle Peter was there, as was his brother Andrew. James and John were at the nuptials, and John recorded the most memorable occurrence at the wedding. Philip and Nathanael were in attendance, although they didn't have as far to travel as did some others, since Cana was their hometown. Thomas, no doubt, made an appearance. Jesus' cousin John the Baptist likely was asked to the festivities, although it's just as likely that he didn't respond. Jesus, in contrast, was invited, and he showed up. But even Jesus didn't receive top billing when John told of the miracle at the wedding of Cana. John begins his narration of the splendid event like this: "On the third day there was a wedding in Cana of Galilee, and the mother of Jesus was there." John knew the fundamentals of good journalism. He led with the information that he felt was most important. "The mother of Jesus was there." John wanted to focus our attention on Mary and her actions.

The Mishnah records that the marriage of a virgin always happened on a Wednesday. The custom was that the bridegroom's friends escorted the bride to the home of the bridegroom, where the wedding was to occur. Once she was in place, the bridegroom went to wherever the bridesmaids were gathered and escorted them to his home to participate in the wedding. Once the bridal party, family, and friends were gathered, the ceremony began. Following the ceremony, there was a great wedding supper.

All of that might sound similar to you in your own cultural celebration of weddings. However, there were some important ways in which the Jewish customs differed from the wedding rituals with which I am familiar. After the supper the bride and groom retired to their wedding chamber to begin their honeymoon, but most of the guests, instead of returning to their homes, stayed overnight at the groom's house. The next day, the party continued. Some of the guests from the first day might go back to their jobs and homes, but others, who were unable to arrive on Wednesday for the wedding, came on Thursday or before sundown on Friday. Once the new guests arrived, another feast was prepared and served. This feasting and partying went on for seven days. And I thought that the rehearsal dinner was a major expense!

A significant part of these weeklong festivities was the drinking of wine. Most of the people of Cana would not have had the chance to drink wine or eat meat very often. The normal diet of the common people of that age was cheese and bread dipped in olive oil, with water to drink. Only at major celebrations would meat and wine be served. That is why weddings were such anticipated events. Families would save up for years to provide a gracious week of feasting and drinking for their newly married children and guests. To receive an invitation to a wedding was a most fortunate circumstance, because there you could eat and drink to your heart's delight and not have to worry about the bill.

About the only thing that could ruin such a happy occasion was for the host family to run out of food or wine. Now you might say, "If Uncle Earl has been eating and drinking at my table for five days, what's the problem if on day six I have to say, 'Earl, you've consumed everything I have. I hope you've enjoyed the party, but it's time for you to go.'" My father developed a saying that he used when dinner guests stayed too long at our house. Smiling, he would turn to my mother and say, "Honey, let's go on to bed and let these good people go home."

If such were the circumstances, it might have been appropriate to send guests on their way. However, let's say that Uncle Earl didn't make it to the wedding on Wednesday, Thursday, Friday, Saturday, Sunday, or Monday because he lived a great distance from Cana. Imagine the feelings that would surface if, after traveling for days and overcoming many hardships, Earl finally arrived on Tuesday, only to find that the wine and food were gone. The situation would be highly embarrassing to the family and very likely infuriating to Uncle Earl.

In this case, Jesus appears to have been the guest who arrived a few days after the wedding party began. Although it is not spelled out in the text, it seems most probable that Jesus arrived on Sunday or Monday, and by the time he made it to wish the happy couple a wonderful life, the wine, as John told us, had given out. The text implies that Mary probably had been at the wedding since the ceremony began. We don't know the nature of Mary's relationship to the bride and groom, but from the way she exercised authority, it seems likely that she was related to them in some way. Whether she was the aunt of the bridegroom, as one tradition holds, or just a concerned friend, Mary sensed the shame and possible anger that were about to break forth on the family of the bridegroom because all the wine had been consumed. So she approached Jesus and said to him, "They have no wine."

Mary didn't really ask Jesus to do anything. However, Jesus evidently heard the instigation in her voice, for he didn't respond by saying, "What a shame. Well, boys, we've paid our respects, so I guess we might as well head on home." Instead, he turned to his mother and said, "Woman, what concern is that to you and to me? My hour has not yet come." The conversation reveals that Jesus and Mary were in on something that had yet to be made public. Jesus was the Son of God, sent to save the world. He possessed wondrous power to accomplish works that would enable many people to believe in him. Jesus and Mary knew this truth. The disciples had an inkling at this point, but only a very dim understanding of who Jesus was. John the

Baptist had only recently told them of Jesus' identity, and the meaning had not yet sunk in.

Mary, on the other hand, had been pondering for thirty years the meaning of Jesus' identity as the Son of God. She too was unclear about what it all meant at first, but she had gained insight over the three decades. And for reasons we are not privy to, she came to the conclusion that it was time for Jesus to work his first public miracle. So she gave Jesus a little push front and center. In effect she said, "Start your ministry now, Son…now."

Jesus replied, "Not now, my time has not come." Jesus used this phrase elsewhere in John's Gospel to indicate that it was not his time to die. Later, during the events leading up to his crucifixion, he stated very clearly to his followers, "My time has come. This is the cup that I must drink. This is why I came into the world." Here at Cana, Jesus knew deep within that it was not time for his death. And at this point in his life, he was not sure what would lead to his death and what would not. That part of the plan had not yet been revealed to him. So he rebuffed his mother's prodding and basically said, "There is nothing I can do about this wine shortage. I know that it is not my time to die."

Mary, however, didn't quit. She turned to the servants and said to them, "Do whatever Jesus tells you to do." Of course, we don't know the exact inner workings of Mary's mind. We can only guess. But it seems likely that she too knew that it wasn't his time to die. She wasn't asking Jesus to finish his work, but she was telling him that it was time to begin. Mary, the mother of Jesus, was fulfilling a very important role. She was pushing Jesus front and center.

I don't think that this interpretation says anything negative about the divinity of Jesus or about his unique relationship with God. Throughout the Gospels people come to Jesus to enlist his services, only to be temporarily put off by the Lord. Two chapters after we are told about the wedding at Cana, we read about a royal official who tracks Jesus down in Cana and implores him to come and heal his son, who is at death's door, and Jesus responds by healing the boy immediately. But on another occasion, two blind men follow Jesus along the road crying out, "Son of David, have mercy on us." Matthew says that Jesus does not respond until they follow him into a house and beg him for healing. And Mark tells us that when Jesus was traveling in the region of Tyre, a Syrophoenician woman begged Jesus to deliver her daughter from an evil spirit. The Lord responds initially by saying that he had to focus on the needs of his own people. Only after the woman aggressively petitions him again does Jesus provide the healing that she sought. In John's Gospel we are told that when Lazarus was near death, Mary and Martha sent for Jesus, and he refused to come. He stayed put for two days, and then he went to conduct one of his greatest public miracles, the raising of Lazarus.

My point is that throughout the Gospels, Jesus often doesn't act until he is implored to do so. Instead, his initial response is to say no or not now, but then he changes his mind and meets the need of the one calling out to him. Haven't you ever said no to something and then almost immediately realized that you should have said yes? Sometimes that is how we learn to recognize what it is we are supposed to do. We say no and then feel an almost immediate, persistent pulse of the Spirit, saying, "You said no, but I need you to say yes."

I think that this is what's going on here at the Cana wedding. Mary has pondered all that she has seen in Jesus and knows that it's time for his ministry to begin. She sends him a signal, he deflects, then she pushes him front and center, and he realizes that she's right—it's time to begin. So he gives the orders to fill the six stone jars with water up to the brim. Then he tells the servants to draw out some of the water and take it to the chief steward (in our terms, the "head caterer"). At some point the water is changed into wine, because when the chief steward tastes it, he runs to the bridegroom and says, "You old fox, you.

Just when I start panicking because we underestimated the amount of wine we need, you break out the good stuff. Most of my customers do it the other way around. They serve the good stuff to the guests who show up on the first day or two, and then when those guests are all pretty well soused, they bring out the cheap wine. But you saved the best for last." Then John says, "Jesus did this, the first of his signs, in Cana of Galilee, and revealed his glory; and his disciples believed in him." How about that—Mother knew best.

John is crystal clear. In no way does he want to leave the impression that Mary had anything to do with the miracle. He says, "Jesus did this." All Mary did was give him a little push front and center. So what is this gospel story telling us? John is letting us know that just as it was Mary's role to help bring Jesus into this world, it was also her role to help get Jesus started in his ministry. He had already heard from his Father at his baptism, when God said, "This is my beloved Son." Now it was time to hear from his mother. Mary says, "Start, begin, do what only you can do in this situation."

Like Mary, it is the role of all disciples to place Jesus front and center. We must be absolutely clear about our mission. It is not to promote ourselves in any way. We are not here to offer the world another institution, obligation, list of rules, voice of condemnation, or religious system. We are here to place Jesus front and center.

The world is beginning to realize that its party is running out of life. We are confronted on a daily basis with the evidence that the planet cannot sustain the kind of lifestyles that our economies keep creating and that millions keep striving to attain. It might not be long before the world realizes that the cupboards are bare and the wine flasks are empty. We must be ready, therefore, to fulfill the role of Mary and tell the world that there is one who knows how to rejuvenate the party with new life, real life, eternal life.

How do we do that? By keeping Jesus front and center. Is our Lord reluctant to take center stage in people's lives? No, but it is true that Jesus awaits invitations into people's lives. Jesus said in the book of Revelation, "Listen! I am standing at the door, knocking; if you hear my voice and open the door, I will come in to you and eat with you, and you with me" (Revelation 3:20). He does not say, "Listen! I'm going to knock the door down, and you'd better have supper ready."

Because Jesus' characteristic way is to await an invitation, we, as disciples, must lift him up to our friends in need and proclaim, "Here is the one who knows the way. Here is the one who can heal your wounds, deliver you from your addictions, lift you out of your despair, and fill you with love." We disciples must be the ones who say, "Is your party about out of life? Are you beginning to see that you have used up everybody and everything that was given to you? If so, let me introduce you to the one who brings abundant life to all who believe on his name." And then, like Mary, we have to turn to our friends and say, "Do whatever he tells you to do. If he says to repent of some behavior and receive his forgiveness, do it. If he says to reconcile with an enemy, do it. If he says to walk away from a destructive relationship, do it. If he says to make worship a priority in your life, do it. If he says to join a twelve-step group and get some help for your addiction, do it. Whatever he says, do it, for he is the one who can bring new life to you."

As Mary showed us, our role as disciples is to push Jesus front and center and let the Lord direct people to do the deeds that lead to life. On April 3, 1968, Martin Luther King Jr. gave his last public sermon, in Memphis, Tennessee, on the threshold of the poor people's march on Washington. This sermon is customarily referred to as the "I've Been to the Mountaintop" sermon. It was delivered to rally forces to stand up for the economic rights of sanitation workers in Memphis.

A major part of the forces that King was trying to rally consisted of preachers. And in the middle of the speech, before he reached the famous zenith at the end, King said to the leaders of the Christian churches in Memphis that he wanted to thank them for standing with the sanitation workers "because so often, preachers aren't concerned about anything but themselves." Then he told the preachers the story of the good Samaritan. King said that he thought that the priest and the Levite passed the beaten-down man on the road to Jericho because they asked, "If I stop to help this man, what might happen to me?" That question, he continued, will always cause folks to pass by on the other side and do nothing. But the Samaritan, King said, asked a different question. He asked, "If I do not stop to help this man, what will happen to him?" King then reminded the pastors that Jesus taught them to ask the question of the Samaritan, not the question of the Levite.[1]

You see, Martin Luther King Jr. executed the role of Mary perfectly. He knew that he couldn't perform the miracle of turning old, watery clergy into Spirit-filled prophets of God. But he did know who could. By putting Jesus front and center, King was able to rally the most timid and self-centered pastors and preachers, and new life was given.

Being a disciple is not about us. We can't save anybody. We can't change the course of anyone's life, and we can't bring new life to a party that has wound almost all the way down. But Jesus can. So let us do the work of Mary, placing Jesus front and center. Then let us say to all who are drawn to him, "Do whatever he tells you to do." When we do that, we will find the abundant life that Jesus promised.

## Questions for Reflection

1. Why did Mary push Jesus to respond to the shortage of wine? How did Jesus feel about her insistence?

2. If Jesus did not feel that it was time to do his first public miracle, why did he let his mother talk him into it? Is it possible that Mary knew something that Jesus did not know?

3. What evidence do you see that the party that we in the Western world have enjoyed for decades is slowly winding down? What shortages do we face? What nonmaterial essentials seem to be in short supply?

4. Do you know anyone whose life is "running on empty"? How can you put Jesus front and center for such people so that they can be drawn to him?

5. How can you assist your friends in doing whatever it is that Jesus tells them to do?

# 10
# MISUNDERSTANDING THE RELATIONSHIP
## Disappointment for the Disciple

### Mark 3:20-22,31-35

*And the crowd came together again, so that they could not even eat. When his family heard it, they went out to restrain him, for people were saying, "He has gone out of his mind." And the scribes who came down from Jerusalem said, "He has Beelzebul, and by the ruler of the demons he casts out demons."…*

*Then his mother and his brothers came; and standing outside, they sent to him and called him. A crowd was sitting around him; and they said to him, "Your mother and your brothers and sisters are outside, asking for you." And he replied, "Who are my mother and my brothers?" And looking at those who sat around him, he said, "Here are my mother and my brothers! Whoever does the will of God is my brother and sister and mother."*

E arly in my ministry I received a call from a local hospital asking me to come and pray for a young woman who was near death. The hospital chaplain had tried, unsuccessfully, to find the dying woman's pastor, and she wanted a Baptist minister to say a prayer with her before she died. I went to the intensive care unit of the facility and was directed to a patient who was surrounded by medical personnel. She was bleeding from her nose and mouth. A nurse moved out of my way and said, "There's nothing more that we can do. She doesn't have long."

I went to her bedside, identified myself, took her hand, and asked God to stop the bleeding and make her well. Following the prayer, I stayed and tried to console her. Within a few minutes her pastor arrived, as well as her grandmother, and it seemed that the room was a little crowded, so I excused myself and went back to my office. That night I asked the church that I served to pray for the family of the woman who had died that afternoon.

The next day, I went back to that same hospital to visit a parishioner who was going to have surgery. As I walked down a corridor, a woman in a wheelchair came rolling out of a room and almost tackled me. She said, "You're the one! You're the preacher who prayed for me." I had not yet perfected my pastoral presence, and so I responded with the first sentence that came to my mind. I said, "And you're the woman who is supposed to be dead." The woman told me that minutes after I left, her bleeding stopped, and that barring any other unforeseen developments, she would be discharged that afternoon. Before I left the hospital, I talked with the nurse who had been treating her, and she said, "We can't explain it, but after you prayed, the wounds that we thought were irreparable sealed up. The patient seems fine."

For several days after that incident, I felt that I had gained entrance into Jesus' closest circle of friends. Thankfully, I never expressed my inner thoughts to anyone, but I harbored a belief that Jesus liked me so much that he was standing by, ready to do whatever I asked him to do. My inflated ego believed that I had the power to convince Jesus to do miracles on demand. That misconception remained in place until a week or so later when one of the saints of our church became gravely ill. His wife called and asked me to come to their home and pray for him. Minutes later,

I stood in the sick man's bedroom and told Christ that we needed a miracle of healing; then I thanked the Lord for doing what we asked. I went back to church thinking, "You did it again." My puffed-up self-image was burst later that night, however, when the man died. In the immediate aftermath of the man's death, I felt intense disappointment with Jesus. Only after I struggled with what had happened for several days did I finally realize that I had presumed things about my relationship with Jesus that simply were not true. Those presumptions had to be corrected if I were to continue to mature as a disciple.

After Jesus began his public ministry, news of his activities filtered back to Mary. Some of what she heard certainly delighted her. The reports that Jesus had healed the blind and the lame probably fit in perfectly with her expectations of how Jesus would fulfill his calling. However, if she heard the good news about her son, she must have also received the more disturbing accounts of his behavior. Surely someone told her that Jesus had chosen a set of disciples who had neither rabbinical training nor significant standing in the community. Mary no doubt wondered how Jesus would establish a religious movement with fishermen, farmers, and common laborers.

We can only imagine the uneasiness that Mary would have felt if she heard that Jesus had asked a tax collector to be one of his followers. That uneasiness would have turned to anxiety were she told that Jesus went to the tax collector's home and ate supper with him, others in his trade, and even one or two prostitutes. Her anxiety would have ratcheted up to full-fledged fear had someone reported that Jesus touched a leper. She had been taught that lepers were unclean sinners and condemned by God. She might have wondered why a man focused on becoming the spiritual leader of Israel would befriend the most notorious sinners in town.

However, the gossip around Jesus' interaction with the sinners would have been nothing compared to the hubbub that surely boiled up after Jesus' confrontations with the scribes. Mark relates that Jesus was preaching inside a home in Capernaum when two men ripped the roof off and lowered a paralyzed man into the house. Rather than scold the men for their disruptive actions, Jesus told the sick man that his sins were forgiven. The scribes were appalled that Jesus presumed to forgive sins, and they told him as much. But rather than defer to their status as religious elders, Jesus defied them.

Mark also reports that Jesus healed a man on the Sabbath of a non-life-threatening disease, in the synagogue, in front of the Pharisees. When the religious leaders challenged Jesus' behavior, he said, "The Son of Man [referring to himself] is lord even of the Sabbath" (Mark 2:28). Maybe it was Jesus' use of that very title that convinced Mary that she had to do something. Mark tells us that the scribes were convinced Jesus was acting under the power of Satan, and they said so publicly. Surely that kind of opinion got back to Mary, and maybe she wondered whether it was true. The Gospel also tells us that people (family and friends) said aloud to Mary what many others in the community must have been thinking privately: "Your son is out of his mind." Although we don't know the precise nature of the reports delivered to Mary concerning Jesus' behavior, we do know that she heard enough to conclude that she needed to use her special relationship as his mother to redirect her son. The Gospel of Mark says that when Jesus' family heard of all that he was doing, they went to restrain him.

Mary caught up with her son as he was speaking to a large crowd. She was unable to make eye contact with him because of all the people surrounding him, so she sent a messenger to tell Jesus that his mother had arrived to have a word with him. The Scripture never tells us what she would have said to Jesus had he given her an audience. My imagination tells me that she might have expressed something like this: "Wait a minute, Jesus, you're really off track here. You need to go back and apologize to the scribes and Pharisees, because you're going to need their support.

Then you have to dismiss Matthew from your followers and completely disassociate yourself from the tax collectors and other sinners you've been hanging around with. Next, go out and find some rabbinically trained sons of community leaders who can become proper allies for you in your pursuits. The friendships that you've made so far are taking your campaign in the wrong direction. And by all means, stay away from the lepers. The last thing we need is for you to get leprosy. No one will believe that you're the Messiah if you get leprosy. Finally, Jesus, your rhetoric must mellow a bit. No more 'Your sins are forgiven,' and please drop the 'I am the lord of the Sabbath' slogan. Those are the kind of words that will just stir up trouble. In fact, Son, they could get you killed."

That may or may not be what Mary wanted to say to Jesus. What we know for sure is that Mary was uncomfortable with the way his ministry was going and wanted to help him find a more acceptable strategy. Maybe she drew the wrong conclusion from the miracle at the wedding at Cana. Perhaps she decided that Jesus' obedience and resulting miracle were signs that she should take over and instruct Jesus about how to be the Messiah. Whatever the reason, Mary presumed upon the relationship that she thought she had with Jesus and went to tell him how to carry out his ministry.

Jesus possibly knew that his mother was coming to restrain him. What we know from the text is that he did not receive her warmly. Instead, Jesus responded to the announcement that his mother was there to see him by saying, "Who are my mother and my brothers?" Then pointing to the followers surrounding him, Jesus said, "Here are my mother and my brothers! Whoever does the will of God is my brother and sister and mother." Mary must have been deeply hurt and severely disappointed to realize that Jesus was not going to honor her special relationship with him by yielding the direction of his ministry to her maternal hopes and dreams.

As disciples of Jesus, we ought to be able to relate to Mary's frame of mind. When we realize how much Christ loves us, it is natural to assume that Jesus will give us preferential treatment. Sometimes we presume upon the relationship and ask for favoritism from Jesus. "Don't let the hurricane hit us," we pray, as if Christ owes us something that he doesn't owe the rest of the folks along the coast. "Help our nation be victorious in the war," we plead, forgetting entirely that Jesus loves our enemies as much as he loves us.

Such sentiments become even more potent when we pray for God to secure a desired job promotion for us, provide special protection for our children, or give miraculous healing to our spouse. Surely we should pray about all these matters, but if our prayers are based upon some notion that Jesus loves us more than the millions of others with similar requests, then we are headed for the same rude awakening that Mary had. Sooner or later we will seek special attention from the Lord and get rebuffed. Jesus, rather than ignore the needs of others to give us what we want, rather than disobey God the Father to make our lives more convenient, will say to us, "No, not this time," and disappointment will descend.

When we pray to Jesus to keep our children safe and then see one of them get hurt, we are disappointed. When we plead with Jesus to restore our troubled loved ones to a healthier way of life and then watch as they slip deeper into danger, we are disappointed. When we ask Jesus to heal a friend who is struggling with a serious disease and then see no progress, we are disappointed. When we see a war drag on and on after we've called out to Christ to bring the conflict to a just conclusion, we are disappointed. It's then we want to go to Jesus and say, "Lord, you're letting us down. You're doing your ministry all wrong. I thought we had something special between us. I thought you answered prayer. I thought you loved me. I thought I was one of your favorites, but you are treating me like I'm just one of the crowd."

William Sloan Coffin writes, "So when in anguish over any human violence done to innocent victims, we ask of God, 'How could you let that happen?' it's well to remember that God at that very moment is asking the exact same question of us."[1] The lesson that Mary learned in this encounter with Jesus is precisely what Coffin says we all have to learn. Instead of presuming upon our relationship with Christ to get him to do what we ask, we have to learn to take our place beside all other disciples and do what Christ asks of us.

Several years ago I had a painful opportunity to learn this lesson. My family had fallen apart, and I wanted Christ to do me a favor and put it back together like it was before. The only problem was that the way it was before was not the way God wanted it. I was immature, hard to live with, and depressed. I didn't want to change in any significant way; instead, I wanted Christ to pacify me by returning the life that I knew. So I prayed, and I prayed, and I prayed. When that didn't work, I promised God various acts of superficial obedience if he would just do what I asked. I was stunned when the Lord did not give me what I wanted. My attitude was "Lord, it's me, your old buddy—you know, the guy who surrendered to the ministry, who went through seminary, who pastors one of your churches, me, one of your favorite children—won't you do this for me?" And God said, "I have no interest in putting your family back together exactly as it was before. Changes are needed."

The disappointment that I felt was so devastating that I ended up in treatment. I hit bottom one night as I played Ping-Pong with one of the male nurses where I was receiving help. I struggled through three games to beat the nurse, and every time he defeated me. During the last game, as the ball hit the floor for the final point, I collapsed to the ground and said, "I can't even win a stupid game of Ping-Pong." I felt powerless, defeated in every way. I had concluded that God didn't care about me, and that I had lost everything that was of value in my life. When I expressed those feelings, the nurse put his arm around me and led me to a seat. Then he said, "You've lost some stuff, and you've been defeated. But you haven't lost what's of most value. God still loves you and wants to use you to love others. You've just got to quit trying to run God and let God run you." His words were powerful enough to help me get over my disappointment and begin to allow Christ to change my life for the better.

In essence, Jesus put it this way: "My true mothers and brothers and sisters are not people who impose upon the special nature of our relationship to get me to do what they want. My true family is composed of the people who join me in doing the will of our Father." As we will see in the next chapter, Mary moved through her initial disappointment to learn this lesson profoundly. May we do so as well.

## Questions for Reflection

1. If you were Jesus' mother, what aspects of his ministry would have made you anxious? What would you have done to express your concerns?

2. What did Mary expect to happen when she went with her family to restrain Jesus? How did Jesus' response to her visit make her feel?

3. Have you ever tried to pull some strings to get someone to give you preferential treatment? How did your efforts work out?

4. Have you ever tried to get Christ to give you preferential treatment? How did your efforts work out?

5. When have you been disappointed with Christ's response to your prayers? What did you learn through that disappointment?

6. What do you think Jesus was trying to teach Mary when he said, "Whoever does the will of my Father is my mother and my brother and my sister"? What do you need to learn from these words?

# 11
# RECOGNIZING LORDSHIP
## The Disciple Matures

John 19:23-27

*When the soldiers had crucified Jesus, they took his clothes and divided them into four parts, one for each soldier. They also took his tunic; now the tunic was seamless, woven in one piece from the top. So they said to one another, "Let us not tear it, but cast lots for it to see who will get it." This was to fulfill what the scripture says, "They divided my clothes among themselves, and for my clothing they cast lots." And that is what the soldiers did.*

*Meanwhile, standing near the cross of Jesus were his mother, and his mother's sister, Mary the wife of Clopas, and Mary Magdalene. When Jesus saw his mother and the disciple whom he loved standing beside her, he said to his mother, "Woman, here is your son." Then he said to the disciple, "Here is your mother." And from that hour the disciple took her into his own home.*

Who made me? God made me. Why did God make me? God made me to know Him, to love Him, and to serve Him in this world, and to be happy with Him forever."[1] Those of you who were raised Roman Catholic will recognize these words as the first lesson of the *Baltimore Catechism*.

What a beautiful set of truths to pass on to every generation. How dramatically different is this teaching from the message that we often give to our children: "Who made me?" "Mommy and Daddy made you to achieve your dreams, to get what you really want, to become the center of the universe, to gather around you all the people and things you need so that you will be happy forever."

My own beloved daughter, Joanna, has been influenced by such teachings. Recently she expressed her worldview with complete openness and naïveté. She sat down at the breakfast table one morning and noticed that it was still fairly dark outside. In response she said, "Look, Daddy, the sun is running a little late today." Joanna believes that when she wakes up, the world wakes up. When she shines forth, the day begins for all creation. She literally believes that the sun rises and sets in her. Therefore, if the sun is not blazing by the time she hits the breakfast table, she is not early—the sun is late. That's okay for a six-year-old to think. It's disturbing for an adult to think that way.

It would be way off the mark for us to say that Mary saw herself as the center of the universe, for certainly she did not. However, as she entered her fourth decade of religious devotion, she did seem to think that she had earned the right to direct Jesus' life rather than be directed by him. Mary began her journey of discipleship with just the right understanding of her role in this miraculous process. When the angel Gabriel invited her to participate with God in bringing Jesus into the world, she said, "Here am I, the servant of the Lord; let it be with me according to your word." Later, when Mary broke out in song, she further indicated her awareness of her proper place in the universe: "My soul magnifies the Lord." Mary started out with a clear understanding that she had been created to know God, to love God, to serve God in this world, and to be happy with God forever. But somewhere along the way, Mary got the impression that she was to serve God by giving Jesus directions. She might have drawn the wrong conclusion from her experience at the wedding in Cana. When Mary pushed Jesus to commence his ministry even though he didn't think it was the right time, the result was a miracle that helped people begin to understand who Jesus was. The success of that endeavor might have caused Mary to conclude falsely that it was her job to give orders to Jesus. As we saw in the last chapter, Mary mistakenly thought that she had the authority to track Jesus down and restrain him because he was conducting himself in a way that she deemed disturbing. *Running the crowd*

If we are honest, we can see ourselves in Mary's behavior. She truly is a model for all that we experience in our attempts to follow Jesus. For at our baptism we all profess to make Jesus our Lord. We all say, "Here I am, the servant of my Lord; let it be to me according to your will." In the immediate aftermath of our baptism, we feel so joyful that we can't help but exclaim, "My soul magnifies the Lord!"

All too quickly, however, we novice disciples reverse roles with Jesus and start telling him what to do. Before much time goes by, our ego starts driving us, and our sense of importance takes over. A life that is supposed to be about knowing God, loving God, serving God in this world, and being happy with God forever becomes a life of trying to use God to get all the achievements, stuff, positions, and relationships that we want. We put ourselves right back smack in the middle of the universe. William Sloane Coffin warns us about this: "There is no so smaller package in all the world than that of a man all wrapped up in himself."[2]

Each of us must have something or someone at the center of our lives. We can choose to put ourselves at the center and live as if life is all about us. That's a hard way to go, however, for it requires us to make the world turn. It requires us to handle everything, to know everything, to protect everything, to make everything run correctly. We grow to think that our opinions ought to be obeyed at work, in the home, at the church, in the community. Why? Because we think that we have to run the world, that we are the center of the universe. We know what is best, we see clearly, we have the solution, we are right.

This thinking inflates the ego, exhausts the human spirit, and becomes extremely dangerous. For this perspective is simply not in keeping with reality. We don't run the universe; someone else is at the center. Mary learned this truth at the same place where every disciple must learn this truth: the foot of the cross. It was there that she heard Jesus say, "Woman [notice that he does not call her 'mother,' as he is trying to help her see a new identity], here is your son." Then she listened as Jesus said to John, "Here is your mother." The Gospel tells us, "From that hour the disciple took her into his own home." No one can know for sure all that was on the mind of Jesus in that hour. Yet it seems reasonable to interpret these words as meaning, "Mary, it's time for you to live as my disciple, not as my mother. Join John, Peter, Mary Magdalene, Salome, and all the rest. Go on home with John and be his mother. Take your place with him and all my followers, and let me be your Lord, not your son."

As hard as it must have been for a mother to heed such words, Mary yielded to Jesus' direction. Mary obeyed her son and made him her Lord. We read about her only one more time in the Bible, at Acts 1:13-14. The writer simply lists the disciples who were present in the upper room on Pentecost: "Peter, and John, and James, and Andrew, Philip and Thomas, Bartholomew and Matthew, James son of Alphaeus, and Simon the Zealot, and Judas son of James...together with certain women, including Mary the mother of Jesus, as well as his brothers." Mary's name is at the end of a list of disciples—not at the head of the list, but at the end. She has taken her rightful place with Peter, James, Mary Magdalene, and all the others. She is no longer the one trying to direct Jesus along the proper path. She is a disciple now, taking direction from him.

This truth might be in evidence in an even more dramatic way in the other Gospels. Only John says that Mary, the mother of Jesus, was at the cross. He writes in John 19:25, "Standing near the cross of Jesus were his mother, and his mother's sister, Mary the wife of Clopas, and Mary Magdalene." Something interesting surfaces when we compare that list with the record in Mark 15:40: "There were also women looking on from a distance; among them were Mary Magdalene, and Mary the mother of James the younger and of Joses [Joseph], and Salome." Mark agrees with John that Mary Magdalene was one of the women at the cross. Mark also says that a woman named Salome was at the cross. Many scholars believe that Salome was the sister of Jesus' mother. If so, then Mark and John agree that Mary Magdalene and Salome, the sister of the mother of Jesus, were at the crucifixion.

According to John, this leaves two women at the crucifixion who are not mentioned by Mark. They are Mary the mother of Jesus, and Mary the wife of Clopas. We could conclude that Mary the wife of Clopas was the Mary identified by Mark as the mother of James the younger and Joseph. If so, this leaves us with an odd situation. Mark names everyone that John names except for Mary the mother of Jesus. Doesn't that seem strange? If she was there, why didn't Mark report this? If she wasn't there, why would John say that she was? And if a writer were to inadvertently leave someone off the list, isn't it much more likely to leave out of the story Mary the wife of Clopas rather than the mother of Jesus?

I believe that the answer to this curious observation is found in Matthew 13:55: "Is this not the carpenter's son? Is not this his mother called Mary? And are not his brothers James and Joseph and Simon and Judas?" Look at the names of the first two brothers mentioned, James and Joseph. Doesn't it seem likely that the woman whom Mark names as "Mary the mother of James the younger and Joseph" is Mary the mother of Jesus, who also was the mother of James the younger and Joseph?

Of course, these were common names, so this doesn't prove anything, but I believe that it's a clue for us to comprehend even further the maturation that happened to Mary's understanding of discipleship at the cross. I believe that Mark had information that eluded John. The writer who had the best chance to actually talk to the people involved knew that Mary no longer wanted or felt a need to be referred to as Mary the mother of Jesus. Read again what he wrote: "There were also women looking on from a distance; among them were Mary Magdalene, and Mary the mother of James the younger and of Joses [Joseph], and Salome. They used to follow him [Jesus] and provided for him when he was in Galilee" (Mark 15:40-41).

I see this as evidence that Mary had been transformed out of the role of maternal preeminence and into the role of one disciple among many others. I am convinced that Mark knew by the time of his writing that Mary wanted to be known not as the mother of Jesus, as John later wrote, but in the way that Mark described her, simply as one who followed Jesus.

This is the journey that all disciples must take. Eugene Peterson observes that every disciple must come to understand what living in the "fear of the Lord" means. Peterson says that the phrase "fear of the Lord" is really one concept in Hebrew. It means that this life is not all about us; it is about something much larger than any one of us: the will of God.[3] Once we realize that our ego doesn't rule the world, but rather God does, then we change from being a person who gives directions into being a person who is humbled at the foot of the cross. We aspire to be known only as a disciple of Jesus.

Once we come to understand that we are not the ruler of our world, but rather that God is sovereign, then our insignificant kingdoms give way to the magnificent kingdom of God and our tiny lives become part of the great God Almighty life. As Jesus said we must eventually do, we lose our lives in order to find them. We quit trying to dam up the life of God and direct it where we think it ought to go. Instead, we take the leap of faith into the pure, flowing stream and allow God's life to possess us and take us where God wants us to go.

Mary started this journey as the mother of Jesus. She grew through many different experiences with her primary identity as the mother of Christ. From the moment of her calling, when she exchanged her agenda for the agenda that God had for her life, through all her insights, setbacks, advancements, and spiritual regressions, Mary slowly but surely was transformed into a mature disciple. The pilgrimage took over thirty years, but eventually Mary reached a depth of discipleship that few ever do. This astounding level of Christian maturity was not demonstrated through a heightened awareness of her own personal holiness and spiritual authority. It did not arrive as part of the benefits of being Mary the mother of Jesus. Instead, Mary became the disciple whom God intended her to be as she set aside her personal prestige and privilege and simply served the one who had become her Lord.

The same is true for each of us. A few years ago I had a dream in which I approached an exquisite banquet table. It was draped with fine white linens. An ornately designed table runner went from one end to the other. Several golden candelabras were positioned at equal intervals along the middle of the table. Beautiful gold-rimmed china plates were arranged in formal place settings accompanied by golden spoons, knives, and forks and crystal water and wine glasses. A magnificent spray of flowers adorned the very center of the table. I sat down at the head of the table with great anticipation of the feast that evidently was being prepared for me.

Suddenly, my eagerness turned to dread as, one by one, my family members began to sit in the chairs along the side of the table. They were subsequently joined by people from my congregation. I began to worry about how I was going to feed all these people. I fretted about whether they would all get along during the meal and whether they would be satisfied with the fare presented. I grieved that what I thought was going to be a glorious gift for me was turning into just one more event that I would have to host, finesse, and manage. As I sat in my despair, I felt a tap on my shoulder. I turned around to see Jesus standing behind me. He very authoritatively said, "You're sitting in my seat."

I don't know if I can fully explain the relief that came over me. I was so happy to get up and take my place alongside all the others at the banquet that I began to weep. Rather than run the show, all I had to do was pass the potatoes, chat with those around me, and feast on the bounty provided. And all I had to do to get that blessing was allow Jesus to take his place at the head of the table.

We may begin the journey of discipleship at the head of the table. We may start out as the one in charge: president of the bank, boss at the office, principal of the school, teacher of the class, ruler of the nation, pastor of the church. However, when we, like Mary, see ourselves through the eyes of Jesus at the foot of the cross, we let Jesus take the place of authority and honor. Then we are released to take our place with our brothers and sisters in a lifetime endeavor to follow Jesus so that we may know God, love God, serve God in this world, and be happy with God forever.

# Questions for Reflection

1. What did Mary feel as she watched Jesus dying on the cross? What would be a mother's natural emotions in such a setting?

2. How did Mary's feelings change when Jesus called her "woman" and then directed her to live with John as his mother?

3. What pain would be involved in relinquishing the role as the mother of Jesus and taking on the role of disciple? Would there be joy in this transition as well?

4. How does the crucifixion give us a more accurate view of ourselves as followers rather than as the ones in charge?

5. If Jesus were to speak to you from the cross, what identity would he ask you to relinquish in order to be a more mature disciple?

6. Are you occupying the head seat at the banquet of your life? If so, what do you need to do to give Jesus his rightful place and take your seat with your brothers and sisters as followers of Christ?

# ENDNOTES

## CHAPTER 2

1. Public Broadcasting Service, Transcript of *American Experience: Fatal Flood,* http://www.pbs.org/wgbh/amex/flood/filmmore/pt.html, 5–6.

## CHAPTER 3

1. M. Scott Peck, *The Road Less Traveled: A New Psychology of Love, Traditional Values, and Spiritual Growth* (New York: Simon & Schuster, 1978), 88.

## CHAPTER 4

1. Walker Percy, *The Last Gentleman* (New York: Farrar, Straus & Giroux, 1966), 8.

2. St. John of the Cross, *The Collected Works of St. John of the Cross* (Washington, DC: ICS Publications, 1991), 360–62.

## CHAPTER 5

1. Wells Tower, "Mysterious Ways," *Washington Post,* 30 October 2005, W8–14.

## CHAPTER 6

1. From an unpublished lecture given by Ronald Rolheiser at Boston College, June 2005.

2. Charles Marsh, *God's Long Summer: Stories of Faith and Civil Rights* (Princeton, NJ: Princeton University Press, 1997), 20–22.

3. Mamie Till-Mobley and Christopher Benson, *Death of Innocence* (New York: Random House, 2003), 262.

4. Corrie ten Boom, *The Hiding Place* (Washington Depot, CT: Chosen Books, 1971), 215.

## CHAPTER 7

1. G. B. Caird, *The Gospel of Saint Luke* (Hammondsworth, UK: Penguin Books, 1963), 64.

## CHAPTER 8

1. Simone Weil, *Waiting for God*, trans. Emma Craufurd (New York: Perennial Classics, 2001), 128.

2. St. Augustine, *The Confessions of St. Augustine* (New York: Penguin Books, 1963), 40.

3. Timothy B. Tyson, *Blood Done Sign My Name: A True Story* (New York: Three Rivers Press, 2004), 288.

## CHAPTER 9

1. Martin Luther King Jr., *I've Been to the Mountaintop* (San Francisco: HarperSanFrancisco, 1994), 15–27.

## CHAPTER 10

1 William Sloane Coffin, *Credo* (Louisville: Westminster John Knox, 2004), 27.

## CHAPTER 11

1. *Baltimore Catechism*, no. 1.

2. William Sloane Coffin, *Credo* (Louisville: Westminster John Knox, 2004), 24.

3. Eugene H. Peterson, *Christ Plays in Ten Thousand Places: A Conversation in Spiritual Theology* (Grand Rapids: Eerdmans, 2005), 40–42.